Chas Newkey-Burden

The Pocket Essential

NUCLEAR PARANOIA

TRIDENT

GW00580193

www.pocketessentials.com

First published in Great Britain 2003 by
Pocket Essentials, P O Box 394, Harpenden, Herts, AL5 1XJ, UK

Distributed in the USA by Trafalgar Square Publishing,
PO Box 257, Howe Hill Road, North Pomfret, Vermont 05053

A CIP catalogue record for this book is available from the British Library.

ISBN 1-904048-22-6

2 4 6 8 10 9 7 5 3 1

Book typeset by Wordsmith Solutions Ltd
Printed and bound by Cox & Wyman

To Chris, who never worries about any of this.

Acknowledgements

Thanks: David Atter, Dennis Bergkamp, Bill Borrows, Chas Chandler, Adrian Clarke, Matthew Collin, Matthew DeAbaitua, Paul Duncan, Kim Fletcher, Matt Ford, Paolo Hewitt, Adam Higginbotham, Sam Jordison, Will Jessop, Rob Kemp, Alan Landsdowne, David Mathew, Eloise Millar, Ion Mills, Clive Nelson, Kim Newman, Zoe Pagnamenta, Julia Raeside, Lorna Russell, Delilah Seale, Mark Simpson, Cameron Smith, Claire Stannard, Mr & Mrs Waller, Shaun Waterman and Henry Winter.

Special thanks: Martin Amis, Paul Binnion, Ali Catterall, Karen Meagher, Barnaby, Mum, Dad, Tristan and Pen.

CONTENTS

Introduction: Things that go bang in the night

'Everyone is interested in nuclear weapons, even those people who affirm and actually believe they've never give the question a moment's thought. We are all interested parties.'

Martin Amis, *Einstein's Monsters*.

August 15, 1945: 'War Over! 50 Years of Nuclear Paranoia Begin Today.'

Headline in satirical newspaper, *The Onion*.

It grabs each of us in different ways but once it's got a grip on us, we can never quite shake it off. Like a nagging headache, it hides in the backseat of our heads and hops into the front-seat at appropriate moments: when we're watching a news report about a war our country is about to get involved in, or when a Russian President is ill in hospital and rumours of a coup begin to circulate. When a plane passing overhead sounds a little noisier than usual or is flying a little lower than we're accustomed to. Or when our local authority tests our area's sirens. Or simply every time we see a photograph of George W Bush or Osama Bin Laden.

Has there ever been, will there ever be a bigger, more mind-boggling thing to worry about than nuclear war? In so many ways, the world seems a more dangerous place than ever thanks to the rise of global terrorism but even during those uncertain months following the September 11 attacks, we never reached anywhere near the white-knuckle fear that was felt during the thirteen days of the Cuba missile crisis.

We watch films and documentaries and read books about the horror of the Nazi holocaust and other key dark shadows across the history of mankind. Nuclear weapons threaten to conclude that history with unpleasant abruptness and when we watch films about their effects, or read about them, we're looking to a tragedy of biblical proportions that has yet to occur. It's the fact that it could indeed occur at anytime, with just three minutes warning, that gives rise to nuclear paranoia.

Which first grabbed me in 1984. I sat down, at the tender age of 11, to watch a BBC 2 film about the effects of a nuclear attack on the good people of Sheffield. Just as a nuclear bomb destroyed most of the city, the film *Threads* blew me away. At that point, I realised that to be killed by a nuclear attack was a horrific fate – second only to surviving a nuclear attack.

I was traumatised by *Threads*. My physical reactions during it, vomiting and shaking, mirrored those of the radiation-struck cast. Following its harrowing conclusion, I sat frozen during the closing titles wondering what was next for me, for all of us. Was it worth carrying on? Speak to so many people who were teenagers in Britain around this time and they'll have a similar memory. The following morning I rang up CND to find out if there was a Youth CND branch in my area. No, there wasn't – so I formed one, handed out leaflets and attended those huge marches in Hyde Park.

But this wasn't so much about politics for me, despite the advice of detractors that I 'just go and live in Russia'. I just desperately didn't want what happened in *Threads* to happen to me. I was utterly consumed by a fear of nuclear war. I was never much interested in the logical, political arguments for and against unilateral nuclear disarmament; I just knew I didn't want the bomb to blow up over England. I wonder now, looking back, how many of my fellow CND marches were more simply petrified than political.

I may not have been au fait with the intricacies of the debate about what we should do with them, but I knew all about the many exotic ways a nuclear bomb could kill you. How the initial flash could blind you even if you were hundreds of miles away from the explosion. The way you would endure 48 hours of nausea, vomiting and convulsions before dying of brain damage, if you received a 5,000 rads dose of radiation in the aftermath of the explosion. How in Hiroshima and Nagasaki, some people melted like cheese under a hot grill while others simply disappeared leaving behind just shadows as evidence they ever existed.

I understood all this. But, given that I knew this, and having watched *Threads* which made me decide that nuclear war was most certainly a bad thing – why did I need to, why do I need to continue to seek out other glimpses of nuclear apocalypse? Why, after hearing that *The War Game* was the most depressing nuclear war film ever and one that made *Threads* look like *Play School*, did I order it from an American website and count the days until I could watch it? Why do I read books, not just for research but for recreation, about the bombing of Hiroshima and Nagasaki? Why do I try and turn every post-pub conversation with friends into a 'what would you do when you heard the sirens start?' discussion?

It gets darker, so much darker when I log-on to the Internet. Christ, I hope no one ever finds out about those pictures I keep looking up. I'll never be able to send my PC in for repair, you know – not with those on the Internet history files. That's right, those mushroom cloud galleries. Picture after picture of the most awesome explosions on earth, they are great for right-clicking and setting as your wallpaper.

My bookcase is so full of books about nuclear war, it would surely send a geiger counter into excited overdrive. Including titles like *London After The Bomb*, *High Tech Holocaust*, *Brother In The Land*, *The Nuclear Age* – it always provokes lengthy and fascinating silence from first-time visitors to my house. Then when we've finished not discussing the books, we can turn to my video collection…

It earns one a very peculiar notoriety, all this. On September 11, 2001, I was unaware of the events in the US for a few hours. Then, I started getting text messages saying: 'Maybe you were right', 'It's the end of the world' and 'Your nuclear moment might be coming'. Then, a few months later, I was sitting on a crowded, but silent, commuter train one morning when an old friend recognised me. 'You must be loving all this,' he said, 'all this talk of nuclear war between India and Pakistan.' Of course, I wasn't loving it at all but I could see what he meant.

I'm not alone. There is something in a lot of us that relishes the thought of studying the end of the world and nuclear war is an enduringly popular scenario. Films like *Dr Strangelove*, *Fail Safe* and *Threads* have devoted cult followings and the nuclear paranoia novel

The Sum Of All Our Fears sold bucket-loads. Lots of people enjoy scaring themselves about the way their life could end and all the horror and gore that would go with it.

Perhaps it's the sheer scale of nuclear Armageddon that does it for us. After all, we could any of us die of bowel cancer and there would be plenty of horror and gore involved in that. The same goes for a motorway pile-up or nasty lawnmower accident. But we don't watch many films, read many books or have many mind-blowing late-night conversations about those death scenarios.

It's not just films and books either; there is no end of nuclear paraphernalia out there. The Bureau of Atomic Tourism promotes potential holiday destinations around the world that have a nuclear link. Yes, you heard that one right. The Trinity site, where the world's first nuclear bomb was tested, Hiroshima and Nagasaki and a host of atomic museums worldwide head the popularity list.

I once spoke to a man who had worked in the civil service on nuclear defence issues during the Thatcher years. Finding a kindred spirit at last, I talked about all matters nuclear with him. Referring to how the nuclear threat had declined with the ending of the Cold War, he mourned: 'Pity, it was all part of the fun during the good old days.' The *good* old days?

Internet websites sell Geiger counters, fallout suits and radiation blocking tablets to anyone stupid enough or scared enough to part with their cash. Videos comprised of nothing but footage of nuclear explosions are sold through Amazon. You could probably spend all 365 days of the year wallowing in nuclear paranoia if you really wanted.

Speaking of years, us paranoiacs even have our own calendar. In one of his nuclear apocalyptic stories, Martin Amis creates his own atomic version of the 'BC' and 'AD' – the 'PN' or post-nuclear calendar, which counts from 1945, the year of the Hiroshima and Nagasaki bombings.

And as we'll see, there are enough pop songs about nuclear war to fill evening after evening of doomsday discos. Our interest in nuclear missies is all-consuming, which is appropriate enough as that's exactly what the missiles threaten to do to us, of course.

The nuclear bomb doesn't just finish your life, it takes everyone else with you. Do we necessarily think this is a bad thing? There is a definite overtone of misanthropy in all of this. If, on balance, you're not so keen on most of the human race you can learn to not only stop worrying about the bomb but positively love it. Perhaps surviving a nuclear war wouldn't be so bad?

It would be a great leveller. Drop a nuke on London and it wouldn't just be Hackney, Brixton and Finsbury Park that copped it. Sloane Square, Westminster and the City of London would also be turned into a pile of ash. Even CND marchers in the 1980s, hardly the biggest fans of the bomb, saw an upside to the very things they wanted abolished: 'Nuclear bombs kill policemen too, doo-dah, doo-dah,' they would sing.

When I interviewed Kim Newman, author of *Millennium Movies*, for this book, I asked him where he thinks the obsession with nuclear Armageddon comes from. 'There is a real attraction in nuclear war and ruined cities,' he said. 'It's actually fun to trash everything, you don't need to worry about everyday things anymore. There's a great simplicity. The frustration of modern life, the thought that if it all went away, wouldn't it be great?'

It would give us a quick dose of perspective. Put this book down for a second and make a list of the five things that you have worried most about during the last seven days. How many of them would continue to be a major issue to you if a nuclear bomb exploded this minute? So you didn't get that pay-rise and your phones just been cut-off because you can't afford to pay the bill. Get over it, the fallout is beginning to drop.

It's the fear to end all fears. Nuclear bombs aren't things that go bump in the night, they're things that go bang in the night and make whole countries disappear for ever. It's not little men in spaceships from other planets, it's no men left on our planet. The only scenario that comes close in terms of sheer scale is the meteor hitting the earth one, as featured in the blockbuster movies *Deep Impact* and *Armageddon*. But nuclear death seems so much more available than meteor death,

doesn't it? Just press that button, Mr President, and we'll all be vaporised within minutes.

Let's not seek arguments for why nuclear war is likely to happen,
let's ask instead why on earth it should not happen? Look at the track
record of the species with its finger on the button: the Nazi holocaust,
famine, plague. Let's remember that Albert Einstein said he didn't
know how mankind would fight World War Three but he knew we'd
fight World War Four using sticks and stones. The 16th Century French
astrologer Nostradamus predicted the bombings of Hiroshima and
Nagasaki but also says that a global nuclear war will eventually kill bil-
lions. He says this war will be sparked in the Middle East. Hello!

But let's not get all morbid, there's plenty of comedy in this topic,
most of it provided by our political and spiritual leaders. As we'll see
throughout the book, the humour contained in *Dr Strangelove* is argu-
ably surpassed by the real-life comedy performed by governments
around the world on matters nuclear. Former US President Ronald
Reagan thought you could fire nuclear missiles and then change your
mind and recall them, as we'll see this was only the beginning of his
eccentric beliefs about nuclear weapons. The British Home Office
claimed you could survive a nuclear war by hiding under a table with a
few boxes and jumpers stacked around it. The Catholic Church, meanwhile, thought we should love nuclear weapons provided they are
'clean and of good family'.

We'll also encounter light moments when he learn all about the men
who did baby-sitting sessions with the world's first nuclear bomb in the
days before it was tested. We'll hear what happened when a classroom
full of pupils in Peterborough were told that Bin Laden had just dropped
a nuclear bomb on Britain. There's also humour of sort in the accounts
of how many times we've come within seconds of accidental nuclear
explosions. It's easy to look back and laugh now, though I imagine it
was more serious at the time.

This book gathers together all the different strands of the history of
nuclear paranoia for the first time. The key historical moments, the
films, the books, the pop songs, the characters – pretty much everything
you need to know about the bomb. It includes interviews with authors

Martin Amis and Kim Newman and Karen Meagher, star of *Threads*. It came about because I kept hunting around bookshops for a book just like this but no one had written one, so I did it myself.

What this book isn't is some sort of a doomsday, end-of-the-world is nigh, scaremongering effort. Much of what we'll look at is in the past. The Cuba missile crisis didn't lead to nuclear war. Ronald Reagan didn't start World War Three. *Threads* was a work of fiction, it didn't happen. Even the new wave of nuclear paranoia that has arisen since the September 11 attacks is looked at critically, with a keen sense of perspective. Mine isn't the last voice you will ever hear.

You will also find no judgement whatsoever on the benefits or otherwise of the nuclear deterrent. It doesn't seek to say nuclear weapons are a good thing or a bad thing. It does, however, argue very strongly that nuclear weapons are a scary thing which is quite, quite different proposal. And one that is surely beyond argument.

1. The godfather: Oppenheimer;
Hiroshima and Nagasaki.

In the winter of 1925, a 21-year-old American student, in the midst of an emotional crisis, fled to Brittany and took long, despairing walks along the cliffs. He was, he later admitted, 'on the point of bumping myself off'. He managed to pull himself back from the abyss, and consulted a psychiatrist. Twenty years later, J Robert Oppenheimer invented a weapon capable of bumping off every man, woman and child on the planet.

Born in New York on April 22nd 1904, Oppenheimer is not just the father of the atom bomb but the spiritual godfather of nuclear paranoia. The story of his invention of the bomb begins in 1939 with a letter sent by Albert Einstein to US President Franklin Roosevelt. Physicists had been aware of the potential military uses of nuclear energy for some years, it was only when Einstein realised that the basic process of nuclear fission was known to leaders in Nazi Germany that the alarm bells started ringing.

Although as a life-long pacifist, Einstein opposed the making of weapons, he was not willing to allow Nazis have the monopoly on such a potentially destructive power. His letter warned Roosevelt of the potential power an atomic bomb could have and hinted that Germany could already be working on such a weapon.

In September 1942, the Manhattan Project was launched – its sole aim was to develop an atomic bomb before the Germans could. The project saw an assembly of manpower unseen since the construction of the pyramids and a final cost of over $2 billion. 'The Manhattan Project' as it was known, quickly became larger than the entire US car industry.

Oppenheimer was the director of the project and it was he who decided on the top-secret location of Los Alamos, New Mexico. Despite being unable to tell potential recruits where the project was taking place, how long it would take or what its purpose was, he managed to assemble an elite team of physicists to build the first atomic bomb.

The pressure and isolation of those involved took its strain as they struggled to perfect the process involved in creating the bomb. Oppenheimer himself became a merciless chain-smoker and lost weight dramatically. Standing at over six foot tall, he weighed under eight stone by the time the project reached its conclusion.

And what a conclusion it was. In the wee small hours of July 6th, 1945, Oppenheimer and his team crawled into a bunker at Trinity, Los Alamos. Nine kilometres away, the world's first atomic bomb was resting on top of the 100-foot steel tower, ready to be detonated.

Weighing in at five tons, the bomb was nicknamed 'the gadget'. It had been in position for a few days, and each night one unlucky member of the team would have to baby-sit it. 'Since I was the youngest and probably knew the firing unit better than anyone else, I had to go up,' chemist Donald Hornig later recalled. 'I took along a book of slightly ribald essays - Desert Island Decameron by H. Allen Smith - so I would have something to do while I was up there.

'They had forecast this thunderstorm, and it started when I climbed up the tower. There was the bomb and me and a 60-watt bulb hanging from a wire. It was about nine at night, and the thunderstorm really kicked up. I would see a flash of lightning and then count -- one thousand, two thousand, three thousand - until I heard the thunder crack. As the time between the flash and the crack seemed to keep getting closer, I thought: 'What if the bomb gets hit by lightning?' The happiest moment of the night came around midnight when my little phone rang and I heard, 'Hornig, you can come down now.'

Physicist Joseph McKibben spent the last few hours before the test asleep at the base of the tower. He had some bizarre dreams. 'I fell asleep about 2 a.m. and dreamed that one of my colleagues was sprinkling the bomb with a garden hose,' he recalls. Then, he was woken and told it was time for the test.

In the observation bunker, Oppenheimer nervously slurped black coffee and chain-smoked as his team prepared to detonate the bomb. One member took bets over the power of the explosion. Others were predicting more grave consequences. Chemical Engineer William Caldes recalls: 'That evening, some physicists got on this kick: 'What if

15

we made a mistake and this thing sets off a chain reaction in the atmosphere?' They were passing the time making calculations about how long it would take such a fireball to hit New York, then London, and then encompass the earth. It was just a brainteaser, but it was scaring the hell out of me.'

At 5:30am, the bomb was detonated and the world changed forever. The dark night sky was lit up by a blinding flash of light, 'like a thousand suns' according to one witness, which could be seen as far away as Texas. Witnesses described seeing gold, purple, yellow, violet, blue and grey flashes within the light.

Then came a blast of heat. Seconds later, a deafening roar tore through the bunker and echoed around the desert. 'Oh, the roar! We all wanted to put our fingers in our ears as the roar started. It was not just a boom. It was a gathering crescendo,' remembered a witness. A huge fireball grew from the ground and rose into the sky, before forming into an enormous mushroom cloud, which rose 40,000 feet into the sky.

Oppenheimer stood rooted to the spot as he watched, and recited words from the Bhagavad Gita: 'I am become Death. The destroyer of worlds.' A colleague came and congratulated him on the success of the test with the words: 'Now we are all sons of bitches.'

Within hours of the test, throughout New Mexico and Texas, public speculation over what had caused this amazing flash of light and explosion was growing rapidly. The following statement was released via Associated Press: 'Several inquiries have been received concerning a heavy explosion which occurred on the Alamogordo Air Base reservation this morning. A remotely located ammunition magazine containing a considerable amount of high explosives and pyrotechnics exploded. There was no loss of life or injury to anyone, and the property damage outside of the explosive magazine itself was negligible. Weather conditions affecting the content of as shells exploded by the blast may make it desirable for the arms to evacuate temporarily a few civilians from their homes.'

The Manhattan Project had been a huge success but Oppenheimer quickly developed misgivings about the beast he had unleashed on the world. He told President Truman: 'Mr President, I feel I have blood on my hands.' Truman handed him a handkerchief and said: 'Would you like to wipe them?' Oppenheimer's misgivings weren't strong enough to stop him from cashing in on his atomic triumph to move on up to some powerful circles. Between 1947 and 1952, he was the head of the Institute of Advanced Study, he also held high office in the Atomic Energy Commission.

In 1953, it all went pear-shaped. He was accused of associating with communists, of delaying the naming of Soviet agents, and of opposing the building of the hydrogen bomb. Although found not guilty of treason, he was stripped of his government pass and sacked from the Atomic Energy Commission.

Although by this time the Germans had surrendered, a new target had emerged for the fruits of Oppenheimer's labour – the Japanese. At an allied conference following the defeat of Germany, President Truman boasted to Stalin that the US had a new weapon on their hands. Stalin replied that he hoped the US would make 'good use of it against the Japanese'.

They did. On August 6th, 1945 at 2:45am, a US air force B-29 bomber took off from Tinian Island in the Marianas. It was commanded by Paul W Tibbets and contained an atomic bomb, which Tibbets had nicknamed Enola Gay, his mother's maiden name. The flight was a fairly calm affair, the crew sipped coffee and ate ham sandwiches. The crew's relaxed state can be in part explained by the fact that only one of them, Tibbets, was aware that that they were going to drop an atomic bomb on Hiroshima.

They were aware, though, that something special was planned. They'd been warned that the plane might be blown apart when the bomb detonated. They carried cyanide capsules in case they were captured by the Japanese.

Meanwhile, the city of Hiroshima was waking up. Its population of 320,000 woke to a pleasant summer morning. Its streets were filled with people walking and cycling to work or school. Thousands of schoolgirls were outside, working to make firebreaks between buildings.

The bomb was primed during the flight and as they neared the target, Tibbets ordered his crew to put on Polaroid goggles, to protect their eyes. At 8:16am the plane reached its aiming point, the Aioi Bridge in the centre of Hiroshima. They dropped the bomb which airburst over the city. Within less than a second, thousands were killed by the heat and light of the explosion. Many were simply vaporised, shadows on walls their only eerie remains. Those further away from the blast were blinded or had their hair and skin burned off.

Futaba Kitayama remembers: 'A shattering flash filled the sky. I was thrown to the ground and the world collapsed around me...I couldn't see anything...When I finally struggled free there was a terrible smell and I rubbed my mouth with a towel I carried around my waist. All the skin came off my face, and then all the skin on my arms and hands fell off.' Another, un-named, survivor who was five years old at the time of the bombing recalls: 'People came fleeing from the nearby streets...they were almost unrecognisable. The skin was burned off some of them and was hanging from their hands and from their chins; their faces were red and so swollen that you could hardly tell where their eyes and mouths were.'

Miyoko Matsubara: 'My face, hands and legs had been burned and were swollen with the skin peeled off and hanging in shreds. I was bleeding and some areas had turned yellow...I saw a lot of people. All of them were almost naked and looked like characters out of horror movies with their skin and flesh horribly burned and blistered...They were groaning and cursing. With pain in their eyes and furious looks on their faces, they were crying out to their mothers to help them. A bleeding mother was trying to rush into a burning house, shouting, 'Oh my boy,' but a man caught her and wouldn't let her go. She was screaming frantically: 'Let me go, let me go. My boy, I must go.' The scene was hell on earth.'

As Tibbets and his crew pulled away from the scene, they saw a huge mushroom cloud over the city. Co-pilot Captain Robert A Lewis kept a log of their experiences, which is an astonishing minute-by-minute account of the attack. His reaction to the mushroom cloud is recorded thus: 'My God, what have we done? Everyone on the ship is actually dumbstruck, even though we had expected something fierce. This was the greatest explosion man has ever witnessed…Just how many did we kill?'

Back in Los Alamos, the Manhattan Project team had celebrated news of the Hiroshima bloodbath. 'Somebody opened my door and shouted, "Hiroshima has been destroyed",' remembers scientist Otto Frisch. 'I still remember the feeling of unease, indeed nausea, when I saw how many of my friends were rushing to celebrate. It seemed rather ghoulish to celebrate the sudden death of a hundred thousand people.'

When the US President Harry S Truman was told of the outcome of the mission, he described it as 'the greatest thing in history.' In a statement to the US public, he said: 'If they [the Japanese] do not accept our terms, they can expect a ruin from the air the like of which has never been seen on this earth.'

Three days after the Hiroshima bombing, a B-29 carrying another atomic bomb took off from Tinian Island, destined for the Japanese city of Kokura. It flew through lightning and terrifying tropical storms during the journey. When it arrived at Kokura, it found that the city was hidden by some heavy cloud and so it flew onto the port city of Nagasaki instead. Nagasaki too was covered by heavy cloud but with the plane short of fuel, pilot Major Charles W Sweeney dropped the bomb. Landing only 2.5 kilometres from its intended target point, the bomb exploded at 11:02 am. Nagasaki is a mountainous region and the hills sheltered much of the city from the blast.

All the same, some 40,000 people died either instantly or soon after the bombing, this total had risen to 75,000 by the end of the year. Many of these were suffering from radiation sickness which took hold by mid-September, 1945. Victims began to lose their hair and then suffered from chronic diarrhoea and fever. They developed open sores and lost the white blood cells needed to fight disease.

On August 10, the day after the Nagasaki bombing, President Truman gave orders not to bomb a third city. As Secretary of Commerce Henry Wallace wrote in his diary: 'He [Truman] said the thought of wiping out another 100,000 people was too horrible. He didn't like the idea of killing, as he said, 'all those kids'.'

In any case, four days later, Japan surrendered. But was this really the main aim on the Hiroshima and Nagasaki attack? There have since been many new theories about why that city and Hiroshima were bombed. Historian Gar Alperovitz argues that the bombs were dropped to frighten Stalin and bring him round to the US way of thinking on the future of Poland and Eastern Europe. Meanwhile, Admiral Leahy, who was US Chief of Staff at the time of the bombings, says the bombs were dropped to justify the $2 billion spent on their construction. 'It was my reaction that the scientists and others wanted to make this test because of the vast sums of money that had been spent on the project,' he says. 'My own feeling was that in being the first to use it we had adopted the ethical standards common to barbarians in the dark ages.'

There certainly had been discussions in the US corridors of power prior to the bombings about how they could make their point but avoid carnage. There were suggestions that they could drop them bomb in a deserted place where the Japanese could witness its awesome power, with the threat that the US would drop such a bomb for real unless they surrendered. This idea was rejected amidst fears that if the bomb didn't work in such a scenario, the US would be humiliated. Another discussion suggested that the Japanese be warned where and when the bomb would be dropped, so innocent civilians could be evacuated. This idea was scrapped when fears arose that the Japanese would simply move all US prisoners of war into the area.

Hiroshima was chosen as a target because it had hardly been touched during the war, so the bomb's awesome power would be clear. The fact it was a flat city made it even more desirable. It was also a port and army base, thus making it a military target of sorts. Nagasaki, as we have seen, was a late addition to the list and was in fact second choice target for the August 9 mission.

Having flexed their military muscles in the most spectacular way possible, the United States felt invincible in the aftermath of the Second World War. They genuinely didn't believe that any other country was anywhere near producing their own atomic bomb. So when the Soviet Union entered the nuclear age, it took Washington by surprise.

An American B-29 on routine patrol over the North Pacific first picked up an abnormally high radiation count in the area. Over the next seven days, more radiation was detected by the West. President Truman was as surprised as most at news of the test. Surprised and devastated. Indeed, many in the US administration simply refused to believe that the Soviets had successfully tested their first atomic bomb and comforted themselves that instead a Soviet reactor had perhaps exploded by accident.

The truth was that the first Soviet atomic bomb, Josef-1, named after Joseph Stalin, was detonated at Semipalatinsk test field on August 29th, 1949. The scientific director of the Soviet's nuclear programme, Igor Kurchatov, had placed wooden and brick houses in the vicinity of the expected blast. He'd also put animals nearby, to measure the effects of radiation. When the bomb successfully exploded, Kurchatov screamed: 'It works, it works!' Very well may he have been so pleased, he admitted he would have been shot if he failed. He named this successful test 'white lightning'.

The starting pistol of the arms race had been fired and the world would never, ever be the same again. In 1952, the US would test the hydrogen bomb and wipe out an entire Pacific Island in doing so. Nine months later, the Soviets tested their first hydrogen bomb. Israel, though undeclared, are widely suspected of having a nuclear arsenal. In 1964, China exploded their first nuclear bomb. Then India and Pakistan joined the nuclear club, Britain and France got in on the act too. Meanwhile, several Middle East states and North Korea are suspected of secretly having nuclear capability.

Since the moment Oppenheimer, as a young despairing student, stepped back from suicide and began the Manhattan Project, we have been on an inexorable course.

There's no stepping back now.

2. We all held our breath:
The Cuban missile crisis and its legacy

'They're nuts. One lady's working four shopping carts at once. Another lady's bought twelve packages of detergents. What's she going to do, wash up after the bomb?'

Los Angeles grocer Sam Goldstad
on panic buying during the
Cuban missile crisis.

If you're ever in Havana, stub out your cigar for a few moments and pop into the Aeronautical Museum, where you'll find on display some shrapnel from the U-2 plane that was shot down during the crisis. The Cuban missile crisis is an important part of world history for most of us, in Cuba it's still on their minds in the present.

The paranoid, defensive spirit of the cold war is still very much alive and kicking in Cuba. Just outside Havana, in Alamar, there are a number of huge underground shelters and all Cuban citizens are aware of them. All citizens are also trained by the Civil Defence Forces in what to do if the US were to invade again. Students at the Havana University have been trained in self-defence and are assigned to specific shelters.

There were few people on the planet who would have objected to having guaranteed access to a shelter during those thirteen days in October 1962, when the US and Soviet Union stood on the brink of war over some missiles in Cuba. It was the scariest stand-off in the history of mankind, the most dangerous fortnight in human history. Two superpowers who had enough weapons to destroy each other and take most of the rest of the world with them, stared each other out while the world watched petrified and helpless.

All nuclear units in the US army were told to load their weapons and get them ready to be fired. B-52 bombers, armed with nuclear missiles, were sent into the skies where they circled, menacingly ready for action. US nuclear submarines headed toward the Soviet Union. As Soviet

General, Anatoly Gribkov put it: 'Nuclear catastrophe was hanging by a thread.' Just a bit.

In the late 1950s, Soviet Premier Nikita Krushchev was talking a load of baloney about nuclear weapons. He claimed that Soviet factories were turning out ICBMS 'like sausages' and that his nuclear missiles 'could hit a fly in space'. We know now that this was all rubbish. In fact, the furthest his missiles could reach was Western Europe and they were proving to be woefully inaccurate during test flights. But then, the US public was very worried – the Commies were seemingly winning the arms race!

John F Kennedy campaigned for the US presidency on a ticket that promised to close this perceived 'missile gap'. Once he took office, he was informed that in fact the US was comfortably ahead in the arms race. All the same, he ordered a build-up of nuclear arms and proudly revealed to the world just how far ahead the US really was. Pride restored.

Then, on Sunday 14th October, 1962, a U-2 spy plane took photographs of a series of missiles in new military bases in Cuba. The CIA blew up and analysed these images and the horrible truth emerged – in Cuba, just 140km from its coast, the Soviet Union had placed medium range ballistic missiles with a range of 1,770 km. New York, Washington DC were within easy range. Indeed, the population of every US city except Seattle were suddenly sitting ducks.

When he was told the bad news on the morning of 16th October, President Kennedy, referring to Krushchev, screamed: 'He can't do this to me!' He was still in his dressing gown. It was a horribly unimpressive start to what became a pretty impressive reaction from him. 'I guess I'd better earn my salary this week,' he said later.

He called together his key advisers, a group who would later become known as Ex-Comm, which is an abbreviation of Executive Committee of the National Security Council. Meanwhile, in the Pentagon, the military top brass held their own meetings. One Air Force chief summed up the tenor of their attitude: 'Bomb the hell out of them!' It was advocated that a no-warning attack on Cuba was the only option - a warning would only give them time to hide the missiles in the jungle.

Ex-Comm's members were largely opposed to this. Bobby Kennedy remembers: 'I could not accept the idea that the United States would rain bombs on Cuba, killing thousands of civilians in a surprise attack. This, I said, could not be undertaken if we were to maintain our moral position at home and around the globe.'

On 20th October, Kennedy announced his decision. A naval blockade would be imposed on Cuba, calling it a quarantine to get around international law. All Soviet ships heading towards Cuba would be searched for weapons and any found carrying them turned back. It was hoped that this would allow Krushchev to back down while saving face. Some 180 US navy ships were quickly sent to surround Cuba.

On 22nd October, Kennedy went on US television. He revealed for the first time to the public the presence of the Soviet missiles in Cuba and explained what the US response was to be. He heaped pressure on Krushchev by stressing that the Soviet had lied repeatedly about this issue.

He also warned: 'The purpose of these bases can be none other than to provide a nuclear strike capability against the Western Hemisphere.'

Krushchev put on a public show of calm but going to an opera the Bolshoi theatre with other key Soviet leaders. But behind the scenes, he was described as being in a state of 'total bewilderment'. He too was receiving a certain amount of hawkish advice, from Fidel Castro. 'Castro suggested that to prevent our nuclear missiles from being destroyed, we should launch a pre-emptive strike against the US,' remembered Krushchev. Although he was against such action, Krushchev did warn Kennedy not to shoot at any Soviet ships. 'If the US insists on war, we'll all meet together in hell,' he exclaimed.

On 24th October, the tension grew. Two Soviet ships approached the US quarantine line, the US couldn't tell whether they planned to stop or not but had given their navy orders to fire if they did not. At 10:25 am, they stopped dead. Despite a jubilant feeling among some US military men that they had faced the enemy off, bad news soon emerged when it was revealed that new photographs showed that work on the Cuban missiles sites had gone into overdrive. These photographs also showed Soviet jet bombers were being assembled in these bases.

After some initially frosty exchanges, the two leaders communicated by cabled letters, which were sent in code, some progress was made in the evening of 26th October. Krushchev promised to not send arms to Cuba if the President promised not to invade the island. The following day, Krushchev went on Radio Moscow to whistle a different tune. He would only take his missiles out of Cuba if the US took theirs out of Turkey, which was ironically enough something Kennedy was already planning but there was no question of him doing that now.

Then some US pilots on a reconnaissance mission over Cuba were fired at by Cuba. Rudolf Anderson, who had taken those vital first pictures of the bases was shot down by a missile and became the only fatality of the crisis.

Kennedy once more called Krushchev's bluff by ignoring the Soviet's second message, in which he demanded the removal of US missiles from Turkey, and instead responded to his first message. Kennedy pledged to not invade Cuba if the missiles were removed. He simultaneously packed off Bobby to visit the Soviet ambassador and tell him that the US missiles would indeed be withdrawn from Turkey in time, but not as part of a deal on Cuba. Bobby arrived at this meeting in a highly nervous state and warned the ambassador that many American generals were pushing for war.

In Moscow, Krushchev was on the brink of panic. When he learned of the shooting down of the U-2 in Cuba and of Bobby Kennedy's nervous mood, he became genuinely scared that hawkish US military figures might force Kennedy to start a war. He went straight onto Radio Moscow and announced that he was to remove the missiles from Cuba, no conditions. The crisis was over. The missiles were removed and, later, the US missiles in Turkey were quietly taken home.

Although it was one of the most frightening periods of human history and the time we've come closest to a nuclear World War Three, the Cuban Missile Crisis actually made the world a safer place in many ways. In the wake of the crisis, the Partial Test Ban Treaty was signed by Washington and Moscow, which banned nuclear tests under water, in the atmosphere or in outer space.

Krushchev was widely considered the loser of the crisis, but he didn't accept that in public. In his memoirs he writes: 'The crisis was a triumph of Soviet foreign policy and a personal triumph in my own career as a statesman. We achieved, I would say, a spectacular success without having to fire a single shot! It cost us nothing more than the round-trip expenses for transporting the rockets to Cuba and back.'

The real losers of the crisis were the Soviet people. Krushchev had never been keen on arms spending, believing instead in that the living standards of the Soviet people were more important. In the wake of the crisis, the pressure for him to spend and spend big on their nuclear arsenal won. Before long, the Soviet Union had a vastly increased armoury of nuclear devices but was spending less on welfare spending.

The crisis dealt a blow to the anti-nuclear movement. Suddenly, the nuclear deterrent was seen to have prevented war and kept the peace. Membership of groups like CND dropped off as a result of this. The Vietnam War, rather than nuclear weapons, became the major peace protest point of the 1960s. It wasn't until the late 1970s that interest in CND really began to take-off again.

In August 1963, as a result of the crisis, a hotline was established between Washington and Moscow on the suggestion of Kennedy. Both sides had been genuinely shaken in the aftermath of the crisis, when they realised how close they'd come to annihilation and how laboured were their communication methods.

Contrary to popular perception, the hotline is not a red telephone. It began life as a teletype machine but is now a satellite system, with a back-up cable running under the ocean. It was first used on 5th June, 1967 when President Lyndon Johnson after war broke out between Israel and its Arab neighbours. Throughout what became the Six Day war, America and the Soviets exchanged 20 messages through the hot-line.

It was later used by President Nixon during the 1971 tensions between India and Pakistan and two years on during further conflict in the Middle East. President Carter made use of it twice during the 1970s, including after the Soviet invasion of Afghanistan.

In 2000, the Cuban Missile Crisis was immortalised in the film *Thirteen Days*. Directed by Roger Donaldson, it starts Shawn Driscol, Kevin Costner and Bruce Greenwood. A fine production, it was suitably tense and gripping. Particularly effective are President Kennedy's regular hallucinations of mushroom clouds and explosion. The film was publicised with the slogan: 'You'll never believe how close we came.'

The only criticism one can make of *Thirteen Days* is that it only really sees the crisis through American eyes. The tension of the film could have been increased by more focus on what is happening in Moscow, and indeed, Cuba. All the same, this film outshines the 1974 TV movie *The Missiles Of October*, the only other film about the crisis.

The crisis was also name-checked in the excellent 1983 TV movie *The Day After*. Two of the characters are lying in bed chewing over the escalating tensions, when one of them says: 'My God, it's like 1962 again…and we were in New York, in bed, just like this. But it didn't happen then, and it's not gonna happen now…people are crazy but not that crazy.'

Bob Dylan's 'A Hard Rain's Gonna Fall' has long been considered a song about the Cuban Missile Crisis, with the 'hard rain' being nuclear fallout. However, a bootleg recoding of a Dylan concert on September 22, 1962, would suggest otherwise. A full month before anyone but Kennedy and Krushchev knew about the missiles in Cuba, Dylan was already singing this song. Phil Ochs, however, wrote a song that is definitely about the crisis – 'Talking Cuban Crisis.'

The hotline exists to this day and is tested hourly, with the US sending a test message every even hour and Russia responding every odd hour. This also provides each side's operators the chance to brush up on their translation skills. The US have sent everything from recipes for chilli con carne to short texts about the psychology of pets as test messages, the Soviets have responded with sections of Russian novels.

May it forever be used in such an insignificant manner.

3 'Til death us do part: The atomic romance of Ronald Reagan and Maggie Thatcher

'I turn back to the Old Testament and the signs foretelling Armageddon and I find myself wondering if-if we're the generation that's going to see that come about.'

Ronald Reagan.

'I regarded it as my duty to do everything I could to reinforce and further President Reagan's bold strategy to win the Cold War.'

Margaret Thatcher.

On August 31, 1983, a Korean Air Lines plane was on a regular journey from New York to Seoul with 269 passengers on board. It inexplicably strayed some 365 miles off course into Soviet airspace and some of the most dangerous skies in the world. Over previous months, the Soviet Union had protested to the United States government about perceived intrusions into this area by US planes.

Picking up this plane on their radars, the Soviet Union scrambled two defence planes to investigate. The Soviet planes went through all the internationally recognised warning signals including the waggling of wings and, as a final warning, the firing of tracers across the bow of the aircraft. The Korean Air Lines plane failed to respond to any of these warnings. The Soviet pilot was ordered to attack the plane, which he did, shooting it down and killing all on board.

The response in parts of America was angry and immediate. Only weeks before, plans had been made for Andrei Gromyko, Soviet Foreign Minister, to visit Washington, in the hope of fostering better relations between the superpowers. In the aftermath of the Korean Air Lines incident, the governors of New York and New Jersey immediately banned Gromyko was banned from landing at any airports in their regions, making him miss his first UN General Assembly meeting for twenty years.

The CIA and DIA (Defence Intelligence Agency) announced that in their opinion, the Soviets had quite deliberately shot down the plane in cold blood, fully aware that it was a commercial airliner posing no threat to them. The US Secretary of State, George Shultz, added: 'The aircraft that shot the plane down was close enough for visual inspection of the aircraft.'

But one man was, at first, ominously silent. Ever since he took office in 1981, this man had given every impression that he would delight in reducing the Soviet Union to a pile of dust. And as President of the United States of America, he was in a perfect position to do so. Waiting for his reaction to this incident was like the time between your Mum telling you: 'Wait till your Dad gets home' after you'd been particularly naughty and the moment you heard his key in the front door.

Ronald Reagan's opening salvos on this incident gave little cause for comfort. He began by expressing 'revulsion at this horrifying act of violence'. He described it as a 'terrorist act', a 'crime against humanity' and an 'act of barbarism'. The Soviets were slow to respond, after all Yuri Andropov was seriously unwell at the time and confined to a kidney-dialysis machine in a clinic outside Moscow. When he spoke he referred the US of taking 'a militarist course that represents a serious threat to peace'.

A few weeks later, the US deployed Cruise and Pershing missiles in Western Europe. NATO then began a series of large-scale military exercises in Western Europe, including one that was designed to practise responses to a nuclear attack by Moscow. The Soviets got understandably jittery. Their defence thinkers had always envisaged that if a nuclear attack by the West ever came, it would be during just such a military exercise. The KGB was put on special alert and air bases in East Germany put interceptor aircraft on stand-by.

For a while back there, things looked pretty hairy. But then the 1980s were a particularly scary period when the world seemed particularly dangerous. Leading this general feeling of dread was the President of the United States of America. Ronald Wilson Reagan took office in January 1981. How we laughed that a former B-movie actor, just a few days short of his seventieth birthday, could become the leader of the world's greatest superpower. When we heard his opinions on nuclear war and the Soviet Union, and the opinions of those that advised him, we stopped laughing and started worrying.

Reagan was a paid-up disciple of a right-wing think tank called the Committee on the Present Danger. He recruited heavily from the groups ranks when he put his foreign policy officials together. Among these lucky appointees was Charles Kupperman, who believed: 'Nuclear war is a destructive thing, but still in large part a physics problem.' Another, Eugene Rostow, who wrote speeches for President Reagan was once asked whether, in the event of a full nuclear exchange between the Soviet Union and the United States, either country would survive. 'The human race is very resilient,' he replied. In case we wondered, just out of curiosity, how we would survive, another Reagan man made it clear. William Chipman, who worked on the US civil defence programme, said: 'I think they [the US population] would [survive] eventually, yeah. As I say, the ants eventually build another anthill.'

But what of Reagan himself? Among his more troubling opinions were that the US could win a limited nuclear war in Europe and that nuclear arms, once fired, can be recalled. He promised to dump the Soviets communist system on the 'ash-heap of history' and boasted that the US had: 'a great deal to offer World War Three'. He described the Soviet leaders as 'the focus of evil in the modern world' and their country as 'the evil empire'.

Reagan's hatred of the Soviet Union was a longstanding affair. Thirty years before he took office, he was president of the Screen Actors Guild and fought against the 'Hollywood Reds' who he felt were acting under orders from Moscow. 'The Russians sent their first team, their ace string, here to take us over.' As President of the US, he continued his campaign, albeit from a more powerful platform. 'We have a different regard for human life than those monsters do. They are godless and that gives them less regard for humanity or human beings,' he said.

Although he considered them godless, Reagan never considered the Soviet Union clueless. He put it about that they had in place a hugely sophisticated civil defence programme. Apparently, much of Soviet industry was based underground in shelters that could withstand nuclear blasts. He also claimed that the Soviets had undertaken huge civil defence training exercises, including the evacuation of their cities. In short, he argued, the Soviets were now in a position whereby they believed they could survive a nuclear war with the West.

No matter that all experts, including the CIA, strongly disagreed with Reagan's claims. The US public now believed that the Soviet Union could blackmail their country. In a crisis, it was argued, the Kremlin could issue a nuclear-backed ultimatum to the US – and back it up by evacuating its people from major cities, leaving the US effectively impotent. This was great news for Reagan and his fellow Committee on the Present Danger men. Within two weeks of taking office, Reagan had already increased the defence budget by $32.6 billion. During his first term, he further increased it by nearly 50 per cent, until it ultimately constituted seven per cent of the gross domestic product.

Reagan also initiated a major civil defence programme for the United States. Predictably, he staffed it with men whose comical views on nuclear war were matched only by their willingness to talk gobbledygook. One such fellow, William Chipman, who we heard from earlier, said: 'With reasonable protective measures, the United States could survive a nuclear attack and go on to recovery within a relatively few years.' Later he added: 'It's very depressing and horrifying in one sense, but if worse ever came to worst, I really think people…would be miserable…No one would ever forget what happened, and I hope to God if it ever happened once, it would never happen again.' Indeed, being on the receiving end of a nuclear attack would make you very miserable.

Not that he was alone in evoking religious imagery. Richard Perle, one of Reagan's men at the Pentagon, claimed the anti-nuclear movement in Europe was the result of a conspiracy by European church leaders. 'I had a Dutch friend tell me that the disarmament campaign has been good for the membership drive in the church,' he said. Perle

31

believed that 'Protestant Northern Europe' was particularly guilty in this conspiracy. 'The Catholic South', meanwhile, was 'solid' in its support for nuclear weapons. 'I refer to it as Protestant angst,' he concluded. But where did the good old US of A fit in among all this? 'We're in the fortunate position of having been through a similar period during the Vietnam era,' he explained. 'We've pretty much recovered from that.'

There was, though, one citizen of Protestant Northern Europe not taken in by this clerical conspiracy against nuclear weapons. In 1976, years before Margaret Thatcher became Prime Minister, she was already speaking Reagan's language. She slammed the Soviet Union for its failure to take part in 'genuine détente'. She said their intervention in Angola proved that they had plans for world domination – and then urged NATO to stand strong against them. The Soviet press dubbed her the 'Iron Lady'. Far from taking offence, she loved the name.

And Ronald Reagan loved her. In one of the most striking political love affairs ever seen, Reagan and Thatcher waltzed their way through the 1980s sharing a passion for nuclear deterrent, free market economics and sharing a hatred for the Soviet Union and those darn peace protestors. It seemed more than a special relationship at times.

Thatcher remembers that when she first met Reagan, she 'was immediately struck by his warmth, charm and complete lack of affectation…Above all, I knew that I was talking to someone who instinctively felt and I thought as I did…From the first I regarded it as my duty to do everything I could to reinforce and further President Reagan's bold strategy to win the Cold War.'

'A world without nuclear weapons would be less stable and more dangerous for all of us,' said Thatcher. The anti-nuclear movement felt that on the contrary, a world without Thatcher and Reagan would be less dangerous and more stable. They became the focal point of CND's campaigns. If you only spent five minutes on a CND march in the early 1980s, you would have chanted 'Maggie, Maggie, Maggie! Out! Out! Out!' and had a leaflet thrust at you, warning of Reagan and Thatcher's war-mongering plans for us all. Most memorable of all anti-Reagan-and-Thatcher propaganda was the mocked up *Gone With The Wind* poster, featuring Reagan and Thatcher in a passionate embrace. 'She said she'd follow him to the end of the world,' ran the poster's slogan. 'He said he could arrange it,' it concluded, with a huge mushroom cloud rising behind the couple. Marvellous.

Writing in her autobiography, Thatcher remembers that in 1982, she was 'concerned about the presentation of our nuclear strategy. I was anxious that the unilateral disarmers were still making the running on nuclear issues'. Of unilateral campaigners, she wrote that they had: 'an appeal in the universities and among those in the media, especially the BBC. Labour councils had adopted the gimmick of declaring their areas 'nuclear free zones'. Although CND had begun to lose support…it remained dangerously strong.'

When she appointed Michael Heseltine as Minister Of Defence in January 1983, an important part of the brief she handed to him was to counter this growing influence of CND. Known as 'Tarzan', Heseltine relished this role, even setting up specific government department for the purpose. According to CND, the M15 spied on their activists, bugged their telephones and sent an agent to infiltrate their London office.

Heseltine himself remembers that he took them on simply by changing the questions. As long as the questions were about the presence of US cruise missiles on English soil, CND were winning. But when the questions became: 'Do you want to go unilateral?' or 'Do you want to be totally defenceless?' he won. He also made much of the left-wing leanings of CND, 'ranging through the Labour Party to the Communist Party'.

Helping him change the questions were a number of pro-nuclear pressure groups that sprung up at the time, including Peace Through Nato. Some of these groups worked simply by providing speakers in debates set up by CND but others were less respectable and thrived on disrupting CND protests and disseminating slanderous material against the organisations and its leaders.

He personally confronted the Greenham Common women, who had set up a peace camp next to the base that held US Cruise missiles, in a flak-jacket. If they continued their civil disobedience protests that saw them try and enter the base, he said, they should be shot. He even pushed new by-laws through, to help crush their protests. Looking back over his career, Heseltine was once asked what he was most proud of. 'Oh council house sales, the defeat of CND, the final rationalisation of the Ministry of Defence, and Liverpool,' he replied. Despite the passion with which he took on his anti-CND brief from Thatcher, though, the pair later fell-out.

Like all lovers, Reagan and Thatcher also fell out at times. In 1983, Reagan unveiled his Strategic Defence Initiative, or Star Wars, programme. Exploiting the huge chasm between American and Russian technology, this ambitious programme aimed to build an anti-missile programme in space. This defensive shield, he argued, would intercept any incoming Russian nukes using laser beams. Reagan expected and received opposition over this scheme from Moscow. He may not have anticipated harsh words from Downing Street, though. But Thatcher quickly cottoned on that a protective shield over the US would leave their European allies as Moscow's target. She was so concerned at the time, when she next visited the White House she had strong words with Reagan. He spoke later of the 'hand-bagging' he received. She also gave Reagan a ticking off following the US military intervention in the Caribbean island of Grenada in October 1983, after the country's prime minister was butchered during a military coup. Grenada was a Commonwealth country and Thatcher ticked him off for this intervention.

Thatcher could never match Reagan's reckless rhetoric on nuclear war. Any US President is aware that his huge country could take absorb a limited nuclear attack and still, in part at least, survive. Britain, geographically tiny compared to the US, had no such luxury. So while her nuclear rhetoric was by no means that of a dove, she left the big, crazy talking to Reagan.

In 1983, the anarchist, hardcore punk band Crass pulled off a spectacular hoax concerning Thatcher and Reagan's relationship. Using cleverly edited tapes of television and radio broadcasts by the two leaders overdubbed with telephone crackles, the fake conversation included an admission by Thatcher that she did sink the Belgrano. It also featured a solemn promise by Reagan to 'nuke' Europe in defence of American heritage.

The US State Department went ballistic, calling the tapes part of a sophisticated disinformation campaign by the Kremlin. The Sunday Times picked up on this KGB propaganda campaign vibe. When the truth emerged, Crass were interviewed by television and radio stations from America to Tokyo and took great delight in rubbing the US State Department's nose in it and asking why their tape had touched such a nerve.

Nuclear paranoia peaked during the 1980s and Thatcher and Reagan pushed it to that peak. But there is a delicious irony behind all this. All of us Westerners who walked around in fear of the big one during that decade were fearing that Thatcher and Reagan were going to cause us all to die. It was our leaders we were scared of, not the supposed enemy of the Soviet Union.

While their fling may be over, Reagan and Thatcher still have eyes for one another. In 1994, during a Gala Dinner for Ronald Reagan, Thatcher gave an impassioned speech to her old flame. She fawned: 'Sir, you strode into our midst at a time when America needed you most… you were unflappable and unyielding… you brushed off the jibes and jabs of your jealous critics.'

So how did Thatcher conclude her speech and sum up how she regarded the man who called the Soviet Union godless, who said he could win a limited nuclear war in Europe, who believed you could fire nuclear weapons, change your mind and call them back? She said: 'You always had the right words, and we honour you for it.'

4. Gimme shelter:
The Protect and Survive leaflet; post-nuclear government and broadcasting plans

We'd really miss the important things in life if the bomb dropped. Deprived of the luxury of television, the general public would be forced to look to more old-fashioned forms of communication, like the radio and luckily good old Auntie Beeb has plans in place for post-atomic broadcasting.

It has transpired that during the Cold War, the BBC distributed a supply of comedy, drama and religious programmes to an underground network of radio stations which would have been put into action in the event of a nuclear war. These 20 underground stations, which were maintained up until 1993, were equipped with tennis tables, iron rations and bunk beds. They were to be controlled from Wood Norton, a mansion near Worcester.

Packed, suitably enough, in black boxes, the supply of tapes was intended to be broadcast for up to 100 days of nuclear war and aftermath. The tapes included the musical *The Sound of Music*. Yes, as in 'the hills are alive'. Pity not much else would be. Also included were *Round the Horne*, *Sorry, I Haven't a Clue*, and *Hancock's Half Hour*. Drama was culled from *The Afternoon Play* and *Thirty Minute Theatre*.

A fair amount of comedy there but in the event of the big one, we would get as many laughs as we needed by reading Protect and Survive leaflets. These civil defence publications, issued by the British Home Office in 1981, aimed to reassure the public that we could indeed survive a nuclear war – provided we built a shelter out of doors and sandbags.

Instead, they became an enduring joke and a gift to anti-nuclear campaigners. All these years, the authorities had told us that nuclear weapons were defensive not offensive. Nuclear war would never happen. Then suddenly we discovered that they were planning for a nuclear attack – and seemed to have extremely loose grasp of how devastating such an attack would be. No wonder that everyone from The Dubliners, to Jethro Tull to Raymond Briggs had a pop at Protect and Survive, as we shall see in other chapters.

The whole premise of the Protect and Survive leaflets were that the public would have ages to prepare for the dropping of the bomb, rather than the three minutes they would have in reality. All we had to do was take a few doors off their hinges, place them against a wall and put a few items of furniture, 'filled with sand, earth, books or clothing' around them then stay in these cramped surroundings for fourteen days.

But what should we take into this high-tech bunker? Most important, is drinking water. The leaflet advised 'You will need enough for the family for fourteen days. Each person should drink two pints a day.' So for a family for four, 112 pints should be taken into this cramped bunker. But hang on, that's not all. 'You should try to stock twice as much water as you are likely to need for drinking,' we are told. Have you ever seen how much room 224 pints of bottled water takes up?

Other goodies to be taken in include a 'notebook and pencils for messages, rubber or plastic gloves, dustpan and brush, fruit juice, a radio, Vaseline, toys and a calendar. The leaflet also helpfully advises: 'You will need special sanitation arrangements.' No shit.

It's good to see that even in the event of nuclear Armageddon, the anti-smoking lobby manage to get their oar in. 'After a nuclear attack, there will be a short period before fallout starts to descend. Use this time to do essential tasks,' advises the leaflet. 'This is what you should do: Do not smoke.' Quite right, too. Cigarettes can seriously damage your health.

The leaflet them moves from the farcical to the positively macabre. 'If anyone dies while you are kept in the fallout room,' it writes, an outcome that seems highly likely if you've followed its advice so far, 'move the body to another room in the house. Label the body with name and address and cover it as tightly as possible in polythene, paper, sheets or blankets. Tie a second card to the covering. You should receive radio instructions on what to do next. If no instructions have been given within five days, you should temporarily bury the body as soon as it is safe to go out, and mark the spot.'

As we see in other chapters, Protect and Survive has been lampooned in film, book and music. Anti-nuclear campaigners delighted in it too, here was evidence at last of the insanity of nuclear weapons. CND produced a counter leaflet entitled 'Protest and Survive'. To wonder whether the advice in Protect And Survive gave us anything resembling a chance of surviving a nuclear attack seems irrelevant and churlish. The point is it all sounds like jolly good fun. And during the three minutes warning before a nuclear attack, light-hearted moments would be at a premium.

As they realised what a spectacular own-goal they had scored with the leaflet, the British government desperately tried to repair the damage with a further publication. You won't be surprised to learn that it simply made matters worse. Entitled 'Civil Defence – Why We Need It', it gave away how stung it was by criticisms of Protect And Survive when it said: 'Even the strongest supporter of unilateral disarmament can consistently give equal support to civil defence, since its purpose and effect are essentially humane.'

It went on to attempt to answer some of the criticisms in the shape of a question and answer session. 'Why bother with civil defence?' was one such question. 'Why bother with wearing a seat belt in a car?' thundered the answer. 'Because a seat belt is reckoned to lessen the chance of serious injury in a crash.' It also attempted to quell fears that nuclear war was likely. 'Indeed, while no war is likely so long as we maintain a credible deterrent, the likelihood of a nuclear war is less than that of a conventional one,' it said. Hmm, that's okay then. It concluded with the slogan 'Civil Defence Is Common Sense.'

A fine and moving slogan, I'm sure you'll agree. Trouble is, one of the lesser-known civil defence pamphlets published in the 1950s had already proven that the opposite was true. Entitled 'Home Defence and the Farmer.' It was a work of comic genius. 'Animals are harmed by fallout just as are human beings,' it informed a nation of farmers. 'Indeed, they would probably be affected more severely because, unless they were in buildings, they would be exposed to the full effect of this radiation day and night.' Even more devastating was the news that: 'It is better not to eat green vegetables which might be contaminated by fallout.' It also warned any unscrupulous post-armageddon farmers: 'Produce (except eggs, if needed) should not be marketed until tested for radioactivity.' Got that, farmers?

Later on, the authors of the pamphlet lose any remaining grip on reality when they chew over some crazy scenarios. 'Supposing there were to be a few months' warning of war, these are some of the things you could do to make your family safe,' they write. Did these people really believe that our opponents would write to us in, say October, warning us they were going to nuke us in December? Yes they did, seems to be the distressing answer.

Civil defence advice in the United States was scarcely less risible. In September 1961, three months after his failed summit with Soviet leader Nikita Khrushchev and a few weeks after the construction of the Berlin Wall, President John F Kennedy had a letter published in a special issue of Life magazine, which assured the American public that if they followed civil defence advice they could be among the 97 per cent to survive a nuclear attack. The advice was pretty much as naïve as that contained in Protect And Survive.

In looking for a comic civil defence equivalent of Protect And Survive in the US, we must turn to the Duck And Cover cartoon. First released in 1950, a year after the Soviet Union had joined the nuclear club sparking panic across the US, it featured Bert The Turtle, a cartoon character and advised:

> 'Bert the Turtle' knows what to do! Do YOU kids? Everyone knows that the Atom Bomb can explode any time and anywhere... perhaps even in YOUR town... Be Prepared and learn to protect yourself! When the bomb hits, you will notice a bright flash... that's your cue... to... DUCK! and COVER!'

Far from reassuring anyone, Bert the Turtle quite rightly became a national icon, symbolising everything that was scary about the nuclear age.

The 21st century deserved a new form of civil defence lunacy and it got it in the shape not of a leaflet or a turtle, but a small tablet. Tablets that claim they can save lives in the event of a nuclear attack went on sale to members of the public – and demand for them in the US and UK rocketed in the wake of the September 11 attacks.

A typical pill, sold by US firm KI4U, contains potassium iodide, which saturates the thyroid and prevents the gland from absorbing radioactive iodine - one of the main cancer risks of nuclear radiation. These pills had already been stored by the government for their nuclear power station staff, in case of an accident. In the wake of September 11, they appeared on the open market, most notably over the Internet on scaremongering websites.

'We receive orders from all over the world, including the United Kingdom and I'm sure demand there will increase,' a spokesman for the KI4U website told the author. 'Orders have increased dramatically since September 11. Even though headlines about the nuclear threat attract customers to us, I emphatically deny that we're in the business of scaremongering.'

KI4U's mail-order website discusses the possibility of a nuclear war, concluding: 'You'll have to decide whether that's an impossible scenario in your family's lifetime, or not. And then prepare accordingly.' It offers advice on the correct dosage for a baby or a pet cat. Despite their protests to the contrary, companies like this are going straight for the jugular with such imagery.

But do the tablets work? Following the Chernobyl disaster, the Polish government distributed tablets to their citizens and avoided the 100-fold increase in thyroid cancer suffered by neighbouring Belarus. But as a spokeswoman for the International Atomic Energy Agency told the author: 'Obviously people are still afraid of the possibility of a nuclear, attack and so there's more interest in possible precautions. We'd point out that there are a number of health issues arising from a nuclear explosion, of which thyroid cancer is only one.' Again, no shit.

So it seems that if the bomb drops, the general public are pretty much finished whether they neck tablets, build shelters out of doors or follow the advice of a cartoon turtle. What of our esteemed leaders, who got us into the mess in the first place? Scary and fascinating in equal measures are the only way to describe the plans that were in place in Britain for post-nuclear government. Peter Hennessy has spent years investigating the intruiging history of Whitehall's plans in the event of a nuclear war. His book on the topic, *The Secret State*, is a fascinating read. He visits the Turnstile nuclear bunker in the British West Country, which in the event of a nuclear war during the 1960s would have housed the British cabinet.

Here he paints a great picture of the War Cabinet, without their families who were not allowed in the bunker, racing West down the A4 as war breaks out. As they arrived in the bunker, they would go down the lift and through the corridors, one of which had graffiti that read: 'Stuck here 4 eternity'. From the war room their, the government would plan any response to the attack the country had suffered.

The Queen, it is revealed, would not have joined the War Cabinet in the bunker because as one insider told Hennessy: 'It made no sense...in case the whole lot were wiped out together'. Instead, it was planned that she would be put on board the royal yacht Britannia which would sail around the sea out of the firing line, until the dust had settled. It would surely be a vintage Queen's Speech at the end of a nuclear war ridden year.

We're all very fond of the imagery of the world's leaders with their fingers on the button. But nowadays, the Prime Minister of England has not just the button but the envelope. On his sixth day in office, Tony Blair was briefed by his Chief of Defence Staff, Sir Charles Guthrie, about his country's nuclear arsenal. Blair reportedly 'went white' as the full details of their awesome power were disclosed to him. But he would have found his next nuclear initiation even harder.

Blair was asked to place instructions in a set of envelopes to be passed to the commanders of Britain's nuclear submarines, which would only be opened by them if Britain was wiped out by a nuclear attack. The envelopes would explain how the now dead Prime Minister wanted his commanders to respond.

According to a veteran nuclear planner who spoke to Peter Hennessy, it could be one of four instructions:

1: Put yourself under the command of the United States, if it is still there.

2: Make your way to Australia, if it is still there.

3: Get on with it and take out Moscow [or the capital of whichever country has initiated the attack].

4: Use your own judgement.

We'll never know, unless Tony Blair has a sudden uncharacteristic urge to tell the truth about something, what Blair wrote in the envelopes, though it is of course fun to speculate that he chose a new option: 'Ring Alistair Campbell, if he is still there.'

5. Atomic Cinema:
Why we love nuclear war films, including
Dr Strangelove, The War Game,
The Day After and When The Wind Blows

What is the attraction? Films about nuclear war are guaranteed to be either extremely frightening, enormously depressing, unbearably harrowing or stomach-churningly gory. There are plenty of non-nuclear films which have one or more of the above qualities but rarely do those films carry the added weight that all of what you're watching could happen to you one day. You could be vaporised, you could die of radiation sickness; you could be forced to have sex with a stranger in return for meal of three dead rats.

And yet films about nuclear war still interest us. We still, in some sense of the word, enjoy being frightened, depressed and appalled in this way. Kim Newman, author of *Millennium Movies*, which examines end of the world cinema, said in an interview with the author: 'For fiction, extreme circumstances always work. There is a real attraction in nuclear war and ruined cities. It's actually fun to trash everything, you don't need to worry about everyday things anymore. There's a great simplicity to it. The frustration of modern life, the thought that if it all went away, wouldn't it be great?'

The first serious film that took a look into the post-nuclear abyss was Stanley Kramer's *On The Beach*, which was adapted by a 1957 novel of the same name. Released in 1959, it stars Gregory Peck, Fred Astaire and Ava Gardener. It is set in Australia, the only continent not destroyed by a nuclear war, as its residents face the fact that fallout will kill them too in a matter of months.

The characters face the impending disaster in different ways. Some take up the Australian government's prescription cyanide pills. One takes part in a crazy car race, with a crash being less of an issue in the circumstances. Two wine buffs mourn the fact that there isn't enough time left for them to drink their way through their stock of port.

Meanwhile, a US submarine, which lands in Melbourne, returns to the US to investigate a mystery radio signal coming from the devastated country. They find nothing but one crewmember opts to remain in the rubble that remains of his hometown. Meanwhile, the captain returns to Melbourne and tries to find a new love with a local party girl, before last life on earth faces the final curtain.

The film ends with the camera exploring the deserted Melbourne streets, before focussing on a banner that flutters in the wind. 'There is still time…brother,' it reads in a poignant concluding message, to a soundtrack of Waltzing Matilda.

On The Beach had a huge impact and was praised for its strong message. A scientist, Linus Pauling, said: 'It may be that some years from now we can look back and say that *On The Beach* is the movie that saved the world.' *The New York Times* observed: 'The great merit of this film, aside from its entertaining qualities, is the fact that it carries a passionate conviction that man is worth saving after all.'

Not all critics were so impressed. Time magazine sneered: 'The picture actually manages to make the most dangerous conceivable situation in human history seem rather silly and science-fictional.' *The New York Daily News* went further. '[It] plays right up the alley of a) the Kremlin, and b) the Western defeatists and/or traitors who yelp for the scrapping of the H-bomb.'

While it has some embarrassing flaws, Fred Astaire is highly unconvincing in his role as a cynical scientist and the acting is often wooden, *On The Beach* remains an oddly effecting experience, taking an interesting angle on nuclear apocalypse. It is also the Daddy of nuclear paranoia cinema as none of the films we'll go on to look at would have been the same, if they were made at all, without it.

And what a poorer world it would have been if we'd never got to see *Dr Strangelove: Or How I Learned To Stop Worrying And Love The Bomb*. Released in 1964, it was directed by Stanley Kubrick and starred Peter Sellers, in three roles. One of the most innovative nuclear paranoia films, it is a dark comic masterpiece.

A US General orders his bombers to attack the Soviet Union after finally losing the plot over his belief that communists have flurodised water to make him impotent. The bombers cannot be recalled so the US President calls the Russian Ambassador to the Pentagon War Room and tries to help the Russian President shoot down the planes. The Russian ambassador reveals that the Soviets have a 'doomsday machine' which will automatically destroy the world if Russia is attacked.

Of the fourteen planes, ten are successfully recalled and three shot down. The lone plane that survives launches a nuclear attack on the Soviet Union. As the film closes, mushroom clouds spring up around the globe to the strains of Vera Lynn's 'We'll Meet Again'.

Dr Strangelove has aged best out of the old school nuclear paranoia films. With only three basic locations: the Burpelson Air Force Base, the bomber and the War Room, it has a tight, claustrophobic feel and of course the basic premise of the film could scarcely be darker. But the film is full of richly comic moments. The President finds one of his men scrapping with the Russian ambassador and admonishes them: 'Gentlemen, you can't fight in here, this is the War Room!'

Most memorable, of course, will always be the President's opening gambit as he rings the Soviet President to break the news of the impending attack. 'Look, Dimitri, you know how we've always talked about the possibility of something going wrong with the bomb…Well, I'll tell you what happened. One of our base commanders…went a little funny in the head. You know, funny. He ordered our planes to attack your country. Well let me finish Dimitri!'

The Cold War paranoia of the time is sent up to great effect. John F Kennedy's 'missile gap' propaganda is mirrored in a hawkish US General's fears about 'doomsday gaps' and 'mine-shaft gaps'. Dr Strangelove himself is a crippled former Nazi officer, whose metal arm twitches into involuntary Heil Hitler salutes throughout the film.

The film was originally planned to end with a custard pie fight breaking out in the War Room but this was cut when it was felt to be too over the top. This was surely the correct decision: the ending of the final cut remains one of the most memorable climaxes in cinematic history. And this is nuclear war, not *Tiswas*.

The world premiere of *Dr Strangelove* was scheduled for December 12, 1963, but following John F. Kennedy's assassination on November 22, it was delayed until January 1964. All the same, the Cuban missile crisis was still fresh in the US public's mind when this film was released, adding hugely to its impact. George W Linden, writing in the book *Nuclear War Films*, remembers watching *Dr Strangelove* shortly after its release. 'The audience was quite silent throughout most of the screening... I, and others, emerged from the theatre feeling subdued and heavy – as though our minds were permeated by sombre pessimism.'

It is often said by viewers of this wonderful film that they do not know whether to laugh or cry when they watch it. In the author's opinion, all you can do is laugh at this comic masterpiece. Of all the films mentioned in this chapter, it stands up best in its own right as a film, and not just as an example of nuclear paranoia cinema.

Adapted from the best selling novel by Eugene Burdick and Harvey Wheeler, *Fail Safe* was released in 1964, and concerns the possibility of an accidental nuclear war. It stars Henry Fonda, a young Larry Hagman and was directed by Sidney Lumet. Following a technical malfunction in the US war machine's control system, an order is accidentally sent to a B-58 squadron. The order tells the bombers to fly beyond their fail safe distance at, which point they are trained to stop communicating with Washington and prepare to nuke Moscow.

As the planes get ever closer to their target, the US President, Henry Fonda, talks to the Soviet leader on the hotline and tries to convince him that what is about to happen is a mistake. With the help of a translator, a Larry Hagman, he tries to give the Soviets enough information on the bombers to shoot them down and avert catastrophe.

As unbearable tension mounts, causing some military officers to crack, it becomes clear that the Soviets are not going to be able to stop the bombers from destroying Moscow. The two leaders discuss their helplessness, The US President says: 'All day, you and I have sat here, fighting, not each other, but rather the big rebellious computerized system.' The Soviet President replies: 'Today, the whole world could have been burned without any man being given a chance to have a say in it.'

Eventually, with all hope of retrieving the situation gone and to prove that the impending destruction of Moscow is indeed a mistake, the US President is forced to allow the bombing of New York as a trade-off. In a powerful conclusion, shots of the bomber approaching New York are cut with images of innocent New Yorkers going about their daily business. We then see freeze-frame shots of these people as the bomb explodes, wiping them out.

Fail Safe suffered from the unfortunate timing of its release, shortly after *Dr Strangelove* first hit the screens. The dark humour of *Strangelove* tended to parody exactly the sort of plot contained in *Fail Safe* – and once you've laughed at a parody of a genre, it's never easy to take it seriously again, let alone be scared by it. Stanley Kubrick cried plagiarism and threatened a lawsuit against Columbia, which made both films, over *Fail Safe*. In doing so, he successfully delayed its release until after *Strangelove*, which premiered in New York in January, *Fail Safe* having to wait until September.

Its makers have since been accused of copping out by blaming the catastrophe so squarely on computer malfunction, thus exonerating the humans who run both countries. At the time, however, the film did cause a political stir. President Johnson opposed its premise and the US Air Force refused to co-operate with the production, meaning footage of all four bombers was actually taken from stock footage of just one plane.

However, with so much of the action taking place in just three settings, the Pentagon war room, an underground room in the White House and the military headquarters in Omaha, the film is wonderfully tense. Not all nuclear war films can cast humanity as the bad guys and in raising the spectre of an accidental apocalypse; *Fail Safe* still packs quite a punch.

Packing not so much a punch but a grievous bodily assault was *The War Game*. This Oscar winning drama-documentary depicted the preparations for and horrific aftermath of a nuclear war in Kent. Commissioned by the BBC in 1965, the Corporation's Director General immediately banned it after a private screening. It was the first film ever banned by the corporation. The film's director, Peter Watkins, claims that the BBC told him privately that they expected 20,000 people to commit suicide in Britain if *The War Game* was ever broadcast.

Shot as a documentary and presented by Michael Aspel, (more 'This Was Your Life' than *This Is Your Life*), the 47-minute film uses non-professional actors to create an authentic, newsreel style. It begins by highlighting the inadequacies of civil defence measures planned by the authorities for time of nuclear attack. Impractical evacuation and home shelter plans are portrayed along with growing panic on the streets of Kent. Then, the attack happens.

Three single-megaton nuclear devices explode in Kent and the scenes of devastation and death that follow are punctuated to dramatic effect by real quotations from religious leaders. 'At a recent meeting of the Ecumenical Council at the Vatican an English and an American bishop said that the faithful should learn to live with, though need not love, nuclear weapons - provided they are clean and of good family.'

More in keeping with the horrific images the viewer is confronted with, is Aspel's observation that: 'The blast-wave of a thermonuclear bomb has been compared to an enormous door being slammed in the depths of hell.'

A doctor in a local hospital reveals that the wounded are placed into three categories. The third category comprises those for whom there is no hope. These are to be placed in a holding section and left to die. If any should not be dead after three days, armed police will be brought in to help the overburdened doctors to relieve the misery of those in the third category.

As the death toll in Kent reaches 50,000, the authorities are forced to burn the corpses. 'It's just like making a big grill,' shrugs another of Aspel's interviewees. Again, armed police are deployed, this time to prevent bereaved relatives from removing their loved ones' corpses before they can be burnt.

The film's conclusion comes as survivors gather in a refugee compound in Dover on Christmas Day, some four months after the attack. As the carol 'Silent Night' is played, viewers are shown a young boy who will be bed-ridden for seven years and then die. A group of young orphans are asked what they want to be when they grow up. 'I don't want to be nothing,' they all reply.

The viewer is left with the following, chilling prophecy: 'Within the next 15 years, possibly another 12 countries will have acquired thermonuclear weapons. It is for this reason, if not through accident or the impulses of man himself, that it's now more than possible that what you have seen in this film will have taken place before the year 1980.'

Watkins shot *The War Game* in four weeks during the spring of 1965 and it was scheduled to air in early August of the same year, the twentieth anniversary of the Hiroshima bombing. However, it was deemed 'too horrific for the medium of broadcasting' by the director general of the BBC. 'I did it purely for humanitarian, not political, reasons.' Sir Hugh Greene said. 'I didn't feel I could take the responsibility for someone elderly or unbalanced being so upset by it that they would walk under a bus.'

(This was, ironically enough, the same Sir Hugh Greene that months earlier had delivered an impassioned speech against censorship to the International Catholic Association for Radio and Television. He told the conference: 'Censorship to my mind is the more to be condemned when we remember that, historically, the greatest risks have attached to the maintenance of what is right and honourable and true.')

Mrs Winifred Crum Ewing, producer of documentaries for the BBC, said: 'Well, I have great sympathy with the BBC, having commissioned The War Game and then refusing to show it... I think it was a stinking film. We don't need these emotional, left-wing intellectuals to tell us we can destroy the world. When I see a film like The War Game, I am ashamed of it, and I think the BBC was quite right to ban it.'

In 1985, as part of the commemorations of the 40th anniversary of the Hiroshima and Nagasaki bombings, the BBC finally showed *The War Game*. Far from greeting this with delight, Watkins was furious. 'The BBC is only now screening The War Game because it believes it is finally safe to do so,' he wrote.

'It believes that the consciousness of the public has been sufficiently diverted, that the concern over the issue of nuclear arms has been sufficiently subverted, to allow The War Game to be finally aired, to be swallowed up in the mish-mash of TV, and forgotten with all the other spurious images.' He also spat: 'I wish I'd never heard of the bloody hydrogen bomb.'

Dwight MacDonald told *Esquire* magazine: 'Were I a congressman, God Forbid, I'd introduce a bill making it compulsory for all Senators and Representatives plus all administration officials whose officers are carpeted to attend a special screening of The War Game. Absence would be punishable by one year in jail or $1,000 fine or both.'

Hailed as 'strong, manipulative propaganda of the most justified kind' in *A Pictorial History of War Films* and 'unquestionably the most impassioned outcry against nuclear war yet... a brilliant accomplishment' by The New York Times, The War Game is the most terrifying depiction of nuclear Armageddon ever achieved.

After some serious treatment in the 1960s, nuclear paranoia only became a major concern to the film world again in the 1980s. *The Day After* was a 1983 TV-movie drama about the build-up to and aftermath of a nuclear attack on the USA, focusing on the experiences of a group of characters in Kansas, Missouri. Directed by Nicholas Meyer and written by Edward Hume, its main star is Jason Robards.

To a backdrop of mounting international tension, the people of Kansas do their best to go about their ordinary business. Denise Dahlberg forthcoming marriage with her boyfriend Bruce Gallatin is causing arguments in her household. Dr Russell Oakes discussing the possibility of a nuclear war with his wife Helen, remembers the Cuban missile crisis. 'It's just like 1962 again... and we were in New York, in bed, just like this,' he remembers. 'But it didn't happen then and it's not going to happen now.'

As tensions escalate, panic sets in. Supermarket shelves are emptied as the public hoard all they can to take into their newly-built shelters and motorways are jammed with traffic as people try to flee Kansas. Realising he and his colleagues are sitting ducks, Airman Billy McCoy tries desperately to flee the airbase so he can return home to his wife.

As the air raid sirens sound, Dr Oakes is driving towards Kansas trying to return to his wife. He is a safe distance away when the bombs hit the city and shelters in his car. Back at home, his wife is killed instantly. Denise's younger brother is blinded by the explosion and takes refuge with his relatives in the family shelter.

Dr Oakes finds his way to the university hospital in Lawrence which is already a scene of chaos and horror as survivors beg for attention. Among them will be Denise, by now suffering from radiation sickness, and her blinded brother. While they're away, their father is shot by trespassers.

The film ends with Dr Oakes cracking under the pressure and deciding to return to Kansas: 'to see my home before I die'. Arriving at the rubbled mess that was his home, he embraces a dying stranger he finds on his property. Back at the university hospital, a doctor has managed to construct a basic broadcasting device and we hear his voice: 'Is there anybody there... anybody at all?'

The film was first broadcast on America's ABC network on Sunday, 20 November 1983, following weeks of build-up. It is estimated that half the adult population watched this broadcast and might have noticed that there were no commercial breaks after the bomb dropped as no advertisers were willing to book space in the post-nuclear world.

Its effect was suitably explosive, though critical reaction was mixed. Among its critics was the *New York Times*, which stormed: 'A hundred million Americans were summoned to be empathetically incinerated, and left on the true day after without a single idea to chew upon.'

Later on, *Threads* director Mick Jackson also put the boot in to the way the film was promoted: 'I'm appalled by this level of sensationalism. Nuclear war is not entertainment.'

There is disagreement about how much of a political message, if any, was contained in the film. *Monthly Film Bulletin* wrote: 'It demonstrates the dangers of NATO's policy of 'flexible response', which includes 'first use' of nuclear weapons,' it said. However, ABC president Brandon Stoddard insisted: 'I don't think audiences will be able to find a political statement.' Perhaps director Nicholas Meyer can tidy this up for us? 'ABC gave us millions of dollars to go on prime time TV and call Ronald Reagan a liar,' he said.

Coming from the same era, comparisons between The *Day After* and *Threads* are often made - most of which conclude that compared to the horrors of *Threads, The Day After* is like an episode of *Play School*. Such comparisons are unfair and flawed. Unfair because the backdrop of impending conflict in *The Day After* is realised with far more tension than in *Threads* and the attack scenes themselves are longer and more devastating in the US film. Flawed because as a feature film *The Day After* has a different brief than *Threads*.

All the same, to a British audience, *The Day After* is always going to fall just short of terrorising us. Indeed, with it's soap opera feel and American countryside setting, it is always going to be seen as a feature-length *The Waltons*, only this time with the cast saying 'Goodnight' to each other for the final time.

Somehow, *Testament*, another mid-1980s US nuclear war film has never got the recognition it deserves. Directed by Lynne Littman and starring US TV movie regular Jane Alexander, is the story of a small-town suburban woman trying to keep her family together in the face of and aftermath of a nuclear attack. It was adapted from a novel, Carol Amen's *The Last Testament*.

٭ Carol Wetherby is married to Tom who disappears after the US is hit by a surprise nuclear attack. She lives in a small Californian town which isn't effected by the initial blast but cops the aftermath. As Carol tries to keep her three children safe, hope and life fades away.

In contrast to those other mid-1980s nuclear war flicks *Threads* and, to a lesser extent, *The Day After*, *Testament* carries little scientific commentary. It eschews mushroom cloud, ruined metropolises, firestorms and the like. Instead, this intimate film focuses on a small family in a small town, trying to survive and is a hugely emotional ride. It also focuses more on the characters, as opposed to the message, than its contemporaries.

If *The Day After* offered little hope and *Threads* didn't even understand the meaning of the word, *Testament* makes up for this. There is only a tiny amount of looting in the film, the town pretty much sticks together as best they can. The children of the town hand in batteries from their toys to be used for a better purpose, meetings are held in the local church. Carol until the end does her best for her children and your heart breaks as hers does.

Kim Newman rates it has the most effecting nuclear war film of the lot. 'It's the strongest nuclear film,' he said. 'It's very low-key and has stood the passage of time better than most. It's probably more affecting to watch now than *Threads*. It's more conventional drama and you really identify with the key character.'

Moving rather than harrowing, *Testament* deservedly won Jane Alexander an Oscar for her performance and remains an important contribution to nuclear cinema.

Another film to take the pull-the-heart-strings approach was When *The Wind Blows*. Directed by Jimmy T. Murakami, *When The Wind Blows* is an animated film based on Raymond Briggs' 1982 graphic novel of the same name. It was backed by Channel 4 but given a theatrical release in 1986. Along with *Threads*, it remains a strong nuclear paranoia memory for those who grew up in the 1980s. The soundtrack includes David Bowie, Genesis, Squeeze, Roger Waters and Pink Floyd.

Pensioners Jim and Hilda Bloggs prepare for a nuclear attack by following the government advice in the Protect & Survive leaflets. Unaware of the harsh realities a nuclear attack brings, they are almost excited at the thought of a return to the blitz spirit of World War Two. They also display a naive belief that the government will make sure everything is okay. They survive the initial attack and are devastated to discover that the milk has stopped being delivered, that their toilet won't flush and that their curtains were scorched by the blast. Even as they grow sick and slowly die, the couple believe the government will sort everything out.

Critical opinion welcomed *When The Wind Blows* the graphic novel with pundits of every political standing full of praise. 'Whatever your politics, this is the most eloquent anti-Bomb statement you're likely to read,' gushed *The Daily Mail*. 'We should all force ourselves to read this grimly humorous and horribly honest book,' said *The Daily Telegraph*. *The Guardian* added: 'Aching with love and bitterness, it is meant to break your heart'.

However, the film has enjoyed a more mixed reception. In his book *Millennium Movies*, Kim Newman writes: 'There is an edge of smugness... suggesting that the more 'aware' elements of society are entitled to a few 'I told you sos' in the event of World War Three... It was not made for people like Jim and Hilda but for radical yuppies who took their kids to CND marches.' *The Encyclopedia of Science Fiction* says: 'It suffers from a certain middle-class Campaign for Nuclear Disarmament smugness.'

Certainly, the spectacular ignorance of Jim and Hilda Bloggs together with the implied knowledge of the audience, how we wince as the couple leave the shelter, drink contaminated rainwater and so on, can be viewed as patronising. At times, sceptical viewers can also wonder whether we are supposed to be balking at the horrors of nuclear war or celebrating the way that the anti-nuclear movement have taught us, the enlightened few, the truth about the bomb. How lucky that we're not ordinary working-class pensioners! They don't have a clue, the poor dears!

Perhaps such criticisms are too cynical. As an imaginative way of teaching the young about an issue that effects everyone on the planet, *When The Wind Blows* is a triumph. Anyone who attended a CND march in the mid-to-late 1980s will have encountered numerous new recruits who credited *When The Wind Blows* as their moment of conversion. It was an inspired moment of anti-nuclear propaganda.

Nuclear power has had its fair share of cinematic treatment too, most notably in The *China Syndrome*. Directed by James Bridges and starring Jack Lemmon and Jane Fonda, it is a powerful thriller about a television reporter who uncovers evidence of malpractice at a nuclear power station. Full of suspense, it's a gripping tale.

Outrageous coincidence saw that just two weeks after the release of *The China Syndrome*, an accident at the Three Mile Island nuclear power plant nearly produced a major nuclear catastrophe (see Chapter Seven for more).

Mike Nichols's *Silkwood* had even stronger real-life connections, based as it was on the real life case. Karen Silkwood worked at the Kerr-McGee plutonium factory in Oklahoma. She gathered evidence of serious malpractice at the factory and was put under surveillance by local police. In November 1974, she died when her car was pushed off the road as she traveled to meet a New York Times reporter. Five years later, Kerr-McGee was fined $10 million for wanton and reckless disregard of their employees' safety.

6. *Threads*:
Everything you wanted to know
about the 1984 BBC film

'In an urban society, everything connects. Each person's needs are fed by the skills of many others. Our lives are woven together in a fabric. But the connections that make society strong, also make it vulnerable.'

Against a background of news reports, broadcasting escalating tensions between the US and Soviet Union in the Middle East, Jimmy Kemp and his girlfriend Ruth Beckett are planning a new life together, after Ruth became unexpectedly pregnant. 'It'll be lovely,' says Ruth. 'I just know it will.'

We see the slow yet inexorable build up to war through not just the news broadcasts but through the preparations of the local council, to whom local power will be delegated when the bomb drops. Jimmy's little brother Michael sees bundles of blankets being delivered to his local school. Jimmy's Dad, seeing an RAF plane fly overhead, says: 'There's something going on, I'm telling you.'

As tensions escalate, panic buying in local supermarkets begins and the cunning shopkeepers raise prices in response. '40p! That's scandalous. They were only 26p last week,' complains one shopper. The neighbours of Jimmy's father Mr Kemp are packing their car in preparation to flee to Lincolnshire. 'I reckon we'll be safer over there,' the neighbour reasons. He goes to check that he's turned the gas off. 'I hope so. We don't want the whole street blowing up while you're away,' says Mr Kemp.

Hospitals are evacuated for expected casualties; motorways are closed to all but official cars, in response to heavy congestion on roads leading to Wales and the West Country. The Protect & Survive film is broadcast showing the public how to build their own shelters. A man stands on a street corner selling over-priced tin-openers. '£1.50 a go! Come on, all of you, £1.50. It could save your life!'

The first bomb explodes miles away from Sheffield but the light stuns shoppers in the local precinct. Jimmy Kemp is at work in his local joinery, Ruth Beckett is at home with her parents and grandmother. Jimmy's Dad is at home, sitting on the toilet. 'Bloody hell,' he curses as the light fills the room. His wife is downstairs but their youngest son Michael is missing.

As a mushroom cloud rises in the distance, panic sets in the precinct, a woman wets herself. Jimmy runs off to through the chaos to find Ruth. 'This is just the start of it,' he warns his friend as he takes off.

A one-megaton bomb airbursts over the Sheffield and the screen goes white. We see milk bottles melting; Mrs Kemps curtains catch fire. Then the blast-wave arrives. Houses, flats and shops are destroyed. Woolworths and British Home Stores collapse. After the blast has passed, we see a milk float burning, figures close to death crawling around the ruined city, a cat dying and a charred hand protruding from a pile of rubble. There are corpses everywhere.

Mr and Mrs Kemp do find Michael – dead under a pile of debris. Ruth's grandmother dies quickly too, followed by Jimmy's mother, Mrs Kemp after some prolonged vomiting. We see no more of Jimmy.

In the film's most harrowing scene, Ruth takes to the streets to look for him. A demented woman staggers up to her asking: 'Mandy, have you seen our Mandy?' Two dead bodies lie charred in a car. A little boy approaches Ruth: 'Mum? Mum?' Dead bodies and body parts lie everywhere. An old lady sits stunned under a blanket outside what was her home, near a dead dog. A ginger-haired woman suckles her long dead baby.

Thousands, Ruth among them, flood the local hospital. Clothing is being ripped for bandaging; packets of salt are mixed with water. Basic operations are being administered without anaesthetic, including a man who is having his leg amputated. Screams fill the air; blood covers the floors.

Mr Kemp and both Ruth's parents die. Ruth joins an exodus from the city and faces the dilemma of whether to eat a dead sheep or not. If she eats it, she risks picking up radiation from it. If she doesn't eat it, she'll die of starvation. She joins a group of men and women who are toiling the barren landscape in a vain attempt at harvest.

She gives birth, to an essentially normal and healthy baby girl, alone in a farmyard as a deranged Alsatian tries to kill them both. In desperation for food, she will soon agree to have sexual intercourse with a dirty man in exchange for three dead rats.

The film then accelerates to thirteen years after the attack. A tiny post-nuclear generation, the population has returned to medieval levels, speak in stunted words and grunts. Ruth dies and her daughter soon becomes pregnant herself. The film ends with her in labour. She flinches in horror when she sees the stillborn baby she has produced.

The impact of *Threads* was enormous and profound. *The Daily Express* called it: 'Brilliant, informative and shattering.' *The Financial Times* wrote of its 'stark authenticity' and called it an 'awful warning'. *The Guardian*, welcoming the three major awards *Threads* received, wrote: 'The bomb exploded over the Sheffield and the long nuclear winter set in. Now the fallout has started.'

On the week of the broadcast, *Radio Times* devoted its cover to an image of a bloodied and bandaged post-nuclear traffic warden from the film. The following issue had several impassioned letters from people who had watched *Threads*. One correspondent wrote: 'This vision of our possible future was more chilling than any science fiction and completely believable when supported by so much scientific fact.' The BBC said it received nearly 100 phone calls straight after the first broadcast of *Threads*, with more than 70 per cent saying they were glad the BBC had shown the show.

The way that scientific fact is presented is an effective part of the horror of *Threads*. Through a documentary style voiceover commentary and a series of teletype captions, the viewer is given a thorough factual background to the horror they are witnessing. Within minutes of the attack, captions tell us that 'Two-thirds of houses in Britain are within possible fire zones.' It later tells us how that ten to twenty unburied corpses litter the country, that cancers and leukaemia are widespread. Similarly, the voiceover keeps us informed about the dangers of the incoming fallout, the horror of the nuclear winter and how the first post-nuclear harvest is a matter of life and death.

CND received thousands of phone calls in the wake of *Threads'* first broadcast and had already produced special information packs on the likely effect of a nuclear war, after anticipating increased interest as a result of *Threads*.

A leading South Yorkshire politician, John Cornwell deputy leader of the county council and chairman of the anti-nuclear working party, praised the film. 'Congratulations to everyone concerned with it. What more will it take to convince the lunatics running the nuclear arms race that they are speeding down a cul-de-sac and taking us all with them?' he roared.

Meanwhile, Roger Barton, chairman of Sheffield's Nuclear Free Zone Committee, said he planned to use show *Threads* to Home Office officials, to prove to them how ineffective their civil defence plans were. He said: 'I believe that the film illustrated the point that we should get rid of these weapons far better than we have ever done. It didn't shirk away from it.'

It was raining in Sheffield the morning after *Threads* was first broadcast but that didn't stop city centre workers from giving their reaction to it to the *Sheffield Star*. 'If that's what's going to happen, its terrifying. I didn't take much notice of CND, didn't understand a lot of it and turned a blind eye. I don't think I will as much now,' was one typical reaction.

A survey of local people revealed that nine out of ten Sheffield residents would rather die immediately than face the consequences of the aftermath of a nuclear attack. Of the people surveyed who had been neutral on nuclear arms before they watched the film, half said they now felt more in favour of disarmament.

The public were being politicised but as Kim Newman said in an interview with the author, the film could have just as easily been produced with an opposite political message. '*Threads* was an attempt to get you to debate the issue - the issue isn't really the end of the world, it's what should we do with nuclear weapons?' he says.

'In fact, it's entirely conceivable that you could do a story like *Threads* beginning not with an escalating conflict but with a basic premise of Michael Foot winning the election, instituting total nuclear disarmament and then our enemies seeing it as a chance to attack and nuke us. The latter half could be exactly the same but the effect would be exactly the opposite. The film would be saying unless we maintain our deterrent, this stuff could happen.'

'It was horrific to watch, though. I remember it being almost unbearable to watch at the time. The trappings of our world were being destroyed in front of us. It started off like a British soap opera and, unlike *Testament*, I didn't feel the characters were particularly likeable.'

Given its drama documentary style, its brutal realism and a number of similarities in the plot, notably the caption on one scene that tells us it is a post-nuclear Christmas Day, there is a lot of *The War Game* in *Threads*. Newman agrees: 'There is definitely a real sense that *Threads* is an attempt to do *The War Game* and get it broadcast. I think the makers of *Threads* looked at *The War Game* and felt they had to update it.'

In common with *The War Game*, *Threads* is not interested in offering images of hope or blitz spirit among the war's survivors. Both films prefer scenes of looting and special courts sentencing people to death. As writer Barry Hines told Kim Newman: 'I can't imagine loving parents...The generation which would follow us would be brutal, stunted both physically and emotionally.'

In our current nostalgia-rich culture, with list shows and 'I Love The 1980s' series, interest in *Threads* has taken on something of a revival. It was reissued on video and DVD in 2000 and has a series of fans websites on the Internet. One such site even featured a '*Threads* Mobile Phone Ringtone', which was the tune of the computer game young Michael plays at the beginning of the film and which his father keeps with him until he dies.

Author Ali Catterall, who co-wrote '*Your Face Here*' the acclaimed guide to British Cult films, says: '*Threads* is a copper-bottomed cult item, no question. It benefited from being broadcast in the days before videos and satellite television were widespread. So there weren't any endless repeats, which diminish any film's impact. By having limited access to *Threads*, it has assumed enormous resonance and power.'

The mysterious thing about films like *Threads* is why they collect fans who want to watch these horrific films over and over again. Newman says: 'There is an enormous comfort in looking at out-dated end of the world stories because they didn't happen,' he says. 'Those cold war paranoia scenarios didn't happen. The idea of Russia and America destroying each other, while not entirely out of the question, isn't really there anymore.'

In an interview with the author, Martin Amis said he enjoyed *Fail Safe* and *Dr Strangelove*, but kept most of his praise for *Threads*. 'I very much admired *Threads*, he said. 'I thought it was a terrific piece of work, that film. I remember Ian McEwan saying, after he'd seen it: "Remember that scene where the heroine agrees to have sex with someone for three rats? Yeah, three rats for a fuck, that more or less sums up the post-nuclear world."'

Karen Meagher, who played the heroine Ruth Kemp, was the first person to audition for the role and as a passionate CND member was delighted to get the gig. In an interview with the author, she said: 'I was so desperate to be part of it, I told the director that whether I got the part of Ruth or not, I wanted to be a part of the film. I was a member of CND and had been on marches. It was something I really wanted to do.'

In researching the part, Meagher studied everything from books about the effects of the Hiroshima and Nagasaki bombings to videos about how Falklands war veteran Simon Weston coped with his burns injuries. Unsurprisingly, all this had a deep effect on her. 'I remember sitting on the top deck of the bus on the way home from a rehearsal, looking around at people on the bus. I'd been steeped in all this information about nuclear war. I desperately felt that I wanted to tell people how tenuous our link with life is.'

By taking part in *Threads,* she had a chance to show people how tenuous that link is. Filming took place in a cold November and there were obviously some gruelling scenes to be shot. All the same, Meagher remembers that an 'incredibly bleak sense of humour' prevailed among cast and crew. 'You just had to laugh,' she says. 'I remember when I was shooting the scenes where I'm working on the farmland, years after the attack. 'My character was heavily pregnant at the time, very sick with radiation and I was wearing these horrible lenses to make it look like I had cataracts. As I came off set looking absolutely terrible, I winked at the lads sitting nearby and said: "See you in the disco tonight, lads."'

She was amazed by the scale of impact the film had. 'It just got so much acclaim and there were even politicians discussing it on television. I've had letters from people saying it had a huge effect on their lives. It's amazing how people to this very day still remember it. I meet young people and they say: 'Oh I saw that! I was terrified by it! I suppose there was nothing glitzy about it so it touched everyone who saw it from ordinary people to the powers that be. When you watched it you felt that it could be you, or your son or daughter on that screen. It was so chilling to feel that.

'It was just something that I took part in that I'm very proud of. Making the film was a great experience, never to be repeated. Although I still don't hold out much hope that mankind will ever sort out the problem of nuclear weapons, hopefully the film made people think. I really can't fault that film, it was superb.'

7. Paranoia pop culture:
The influence of the bomb on
music, literature, television and fashion

Some of us had long suspected it, but it took a band as outrageous as Frankie Goes To Hollywood to come right out and say it. They'd already outraged us by telling us to relax when we want to come and had their single banned by the BBC for their trouble. How could they follow this up? By suggesting that the superpowers got sexual kicks from their nuclear arsenals, that's how.

As we keep seeing, the 1980s was surely the decade of nuclear paranoia – and *Two Tribes* by Frankie Goes To Hollywood was the soundtrack to our worst fears. With it's catchy chorus: 'When two tribes go to war/ A point is all you can score,' it bought fear, along with a high-speed rhythm to the dance-floors of England.

Most chilling of all, was the voiceover by Patrick Allen with his Orwellian instructions as to how to avoid death when the bomb drops. Taken directly from the government's 1975 'Protect & Survive' video, his authoratively, darkly delivered words were: 'When you hear the air attack warning, you and your family must take cover at once. Do not stay out of doors. If you are caught in the open, lie down... If your grandmother or any other member of your family should die whilst in the shelter, put them outside, but remember to tag them first for identification purposes.'

Released in June 1984, *Two Tribes* stayed at number one for nine weeks and sold over a million copies. The single's excellent video, directed by Godley and Creme, depicts the US and Soviet Presidents lawlessly scrapping in a small arena, watched by and eventually joined by the rest of the world. As the song played out, Allen's voice returned to warn us: 'Mine is the last voice you will ever hear.' Chilling. Together with their cover of Edwin Star's *War*, this song made Frankie the kings of paranoia pop.

Not that Frankie were alone during the 1980s in singing about nuclear Armageddon. Remember Berlin pop band Nena and *99 Red Ballons*? It's beautiful innocent melody takes on a sinister overtone when you realise the song is concerned about the accidental triggering of a nuclear war. A boy and a girl innocently release some red balloons and confusion over what these flying objects are triggers a nuclear war. 'It's all over and I'm standing pretty/In this dust that was a city,' conclude the lyrics.

Nuclear paranoia soon caught on in the pop scene and for a while was rather fashionable. Before long, Sting was reminding us that 'Russians love their children too,' Prince was pleading: 'Ronnie, Talk To Russia'. Even Def Leppard, Billy Joel and Depeche Mode got in on the act! Nuclear paranoia also got cameo mentions in the work of Duran Duran, Ultravox and The Smiths and a host of other artists.

Although the 1980s were the peak of paranoia pop, there were older, (and frequently more musically credible precedents). During the 1960s, Bob Dylan sang *A Hard Rain's Gonna Fall* after the Cuban Missile Crisis, while Phil Ochs sang a number of nuclear tunes including *The Thresher*. Then, in the 1970s Creedence Clear Water Revival, *It Came Out Of The Sky*, and The Clash, *London Calling*, *Armageddieon Time* and *Ivan Meets GI Joe*, also had the topic on their mind.

One artist who has maintained an interest in nuclear politics is Paul Weller. From 1980, when he barked about buying 'nuclear textbooks for atomic crimes' and seeing 'kidney machines replaced by rockets and guns', his interest was born. Once he had split The Jam to form the Style Council, he took a more direct interest, attending CND marches, playing CND benefits and forming Red Wedge, the musical collective of left-wing musicians.

Cruelly under-mentioned in discussions about paranoia pop is Jethro Tull's excellent *Protect & Survive*, which lampoons the British government's civil defence pamphlet. 'They said Protect & Survive, but our postman didn't call,' it begins, concluding chillingly: 'Burnt shadow printed on the road, now there's nothing there at all. They said: protect and you'll survive.' Two other bands sneering at the same target were Big Country, *1,000 Stars*, and The Dubliners, *Protect & Survive*.

Although it's had a great representation in the world of pop and rock music, nuclear paranoia has rarely got the literary representation it deserves. Any book that could convey the same tension, terror and horror of films like *Threads* would surely be onto a winner. Instead, we've largely been offered blockbusters, horror or sci-fi novels.

Tom Clancy, the main man of the blockbuster techno-thriller market, wrote one of the most famous works of nuclear fiction ever in *The Sum Of All Fears*. In the Middle East, a nuclear weapon falls into the hands of terrorists and is planted on American soil in the midst of growing tensions between the US and Soviet Union. With his famous Jack Ryan character in the forefront of the tale, *The Sum Of All Fears* is classic Clancy. His fans adore it, those that 'don't get' his work will find it oppressively technical, tiresomely long and ultimately bewildering.

Arc Light, by Eric L Harry, is pretty much in the Tom Clancy camp of nuclear fiction, though on a less ambitious scale. The story of how a Russian attack on China turns into a war between the US and Russia, it keeps its focus very much on the experiences of the political and military leaders, rather than the consequences for the civilian populations. It's also heavy on technical detail, which though impressive can become intimidating and tiresome. All the same, the tension is incredible and the final twist surprising.

Domain, by James Herbert, on the other hand begins with the bomb dropping. Set in London, it focuses on a small band of survivors and their life first in the bunker, then in what remains of the outside world. It's gory; witness the huge rodents and graphic descriptions of death, destruction and gore. It also has moments of dark comedy, which Herbert pulls off with reasonable success. All the same, you suspect that fifteen-year-old boys who pick their nose a lot are the true target here.

More enjoyable and interesting is the influence of nuclear paranoia on the work of England's finest current novelist Martin Amis. Although more famed for his phobia of dentists, Amis also harbours a longstanding fear of and obsession with nuclear weapons. One of his best-selling novels, *London Fields*, is a murder story set against a backdrop of a global nuclear stockpile and impending apocalypse. Nuclear war also enjoys further name-checks in his novels *Time's Arrow*, *The Informa-*

tion and, most notably, in his collection of short stories set in a post nuclear holocaust world - *Einstein's Monsters*. There's a running interest at work here.

'I was born on 25 August 1949,' he writes in the polemical introduction to *Einstein's Monsters*, perhaps the finest piece of writing on nuclear paranoia ever. 'Four days later, the Russians successfully tested their first atom bomb, and deterrence was in place. So I had those four carefree days, which is more than my juniors ever had... I am sick of them - I am sick of nuclear weapons... They make me feel as if a child of mine has been out too long, much too long and already it is getting dark.'

'The best time to deal with a nuclear missile is when it is on the ground and subject to negotiation - or, more generally, to diplomacy,' he wrote when opposing the 'Star Wars' initiative. 'The worst time to deal with a nuclear missile is when it is heading towards you at four miles a second. In the latter case, there is likely to be only one winner: the nuclear missile.'

In an interview with the author, Amis explained the difficulties of writing fiction about nuclear war. 'It's sort of everything and nothing, isn't it?' he said. 'As Oppenheimer said, nuclear weapons are shit, they're nothing. In their inert state they are certainly food for paranoia but it's unimaginable, it's never transferred into real life. We've only had two incidents of nuclear use in human history and that was more than half a century ago. They have to be imagined because they hide their faces, they're invisible.

'So in fiction it has proved a very hard thing to do. Every other science fiction novel for many years was set in a post-nuclear world. It seems a common starting point for science fiction novels but it's resistant to artistic literary treatment, it seems.

'Why are people attracted to these stories? Well, I think the human fascination with violence. There's never been anything as violent as nuclear weapons, has there? It's odd that people don't think about nuclear weapons in terms of violence so much as just the end of everything, or an abyss, or going over some sort of line. But in fact we know the line and it's violence – and this is just a greater and more concentrated form of violence than we've ever known before.'

He spoke of the difference between the nuclear scene now and when he wrote *Einstein's Monsters*. 'Back then, people were very scared, partly because of the size of the arsenals and Ronald Reagan's confrontational policy of building up and spending on arms, together with his aggressive rhetoric about the evil empire. Deep down, the feeling was always that nuclear war couldn't not happen. It was so wired in and so many preparations had been made that an institutional inevitability would take over.

'The landscape has changed entirely now. As I said, we're through with the era of mutual assured destruction and we're now in the era of proliferation. It's not apocalyptic fear but fear of a disaster of uncertain scale. It's interesting to see, more than interesting, to see this all being played starting from scratch in the Indian sub-continent. I think nuclear war is only possible now between India and Pakistan. I can see nuclear use now but not a nuclear war, apart from in that region.'

Not everyone has been impressed by Amis's nuclear paranoia. Remembering the mid-1980s dawn of his obsession, columnist Julie Burchill sneers: 'Martin, bless him, had just discovered these really nasty things called nuclear weapons.' Amis clashed with his father Kingsley on the subject. 'I am reliably ruder to my father on the subject of nuclear weapons than on any other, ruder than I have been to him since my teenage years,' he wrote. Kingsley scoffed: 'He's gone all lefty. He's bright but a fucking fool.'

But then, we could all have been forgiven for going all lefty during the 1980s, such was the level of anti-nuclear propaganda flying about. Even school children weren't safe, as Robert Swindells' book *Brother In The Land*, first published in 1984 and aimed at Britain's teenagers, demonstrates. Pupils across the UK were handed this book during the 1980s by English teachers, many of whom were paid up members of CND. The story of Danny, a young boy who survives a nuclear attack on England and the struggle to stay alive in the aftermath, it was a definite anti-nuclear message. Indeed, at times that message was delivered with all the subtlety of a nuclear bomb.

Within minutes of the bomb dropping, Danny remembers: 'A teacher brought this book to school once, Protect and Survive or some such title. It reckoned to tell what would happen if the H-Bombs fell on Britain. It was pretty horrible, but it didn't tell the half of it.' Soon, he writes: 'As I reached the ditch it started to drizzle and something I'd read; a phrase, flashed across my mind. Black rain. After they'd dropped the bomb on Hiroshima it rained, and the rain brought down all the radioactive dust from the atmosphere. Thousands of people from the outskirts of the city, who'd survived the actual explosion, got rained on by this stuff and died of radiation sickness.'

It comes as precious little surprise that in Robert Swindells' biography it lists his interests as 'being an active member of the Peace Movement', though perhaps his teenage membership of the RAF is less expected. *Brother In The Land* was the winner of The Other Award for 1984 and along with *When The Wind Blows*, undoubtedly bolstered the Youth CND membership numbers in mid-1980s.

We've already dealt with the key moments of nuclear television such as *Threads* but how else has our fear of the bomb influenced the small screen? It is perhaps in the world of comedy that it has shown itself most memorably. In 1986, in an episode of the excellent political comedy Yes Prime Minister, called The Grand Design, newly elected Prime Minister Jim Hacker visits the Ministry of Defence and is shown the nuclear button. He is told that the longest that the present British armed forces could hold out against the Russians would be 72 hours. This would, he is told, give him 12 hours to decide whether to press the button in the event of war.

He then has the following typically witty exchange with one of his civil servants, Sir Humphrey:

Sir Humphrey: 'With Trident we could obliterate the whole of Eastern Europe.'
Jim Hacker: 'I don't want to obliterate the whole of Eastern Europe.'
Sir Humphrey: 'It's a deterrent.'
Jim Hacker: 'It's a bluff. I probably wouldn't use it.'
Sir Humphrey: 'Yes, but they don't know that you probably wouldn't.'

Jim Hacker: 'They probably do.'

Sir Humphrey: 'Yes, they probably know that you probably wouldn't. But they can't certainly know.'

Jim Hacker: 'They probably certainly know that I probably wouldn't.'

Sir Humphrey: 'Yes, but even though they probably certainly know that you probably wouldn't, they don't certainly know that, although you probably wouldn't, there is no probability that you certainly would.'

This exchange summed up accurately and hilariously the folly of nuclear deterrence, and another classic British sitcom of the 1980s similarly took to pieces the farce of Protect and Survive. (One could almost feel sorry for the poor sods who produced that pamphlet, couldn't one? Okay, maybe not then.) In an episode of *The Young Ones* entitled 'Bomb', a nuclear bomb appears in the kitchen that the students share. This leads to the following exchange, sending up the Protect & Survive leaflet.

NEIL: Seriously, we ought to do something about this bomb! I'm going upstairs to get the incredibly helpful and informative 'Protect and Survive' manual! Nobody better touch this while I'm gone!

RICK: What are you doing?

[Neil is reading his survival manual while painting himself white with a paintbrush]

NEIL: Oh, painting myself white to deflect the blast!

RICK: That's great, isn't it, Racial discrimination, even in death! What are these? [indicates a few lunchbags on the table]

NEIL: Oh, sandbags!

[The table now has a drape over it saying, 'KEEP OUT, FALLOUT'. Mike enters carrying food in both hands]

MIKE: Neil, where's the table?

NEIL: Oh, good. You got the provisions.

MIKE: Yeah

NEIL: No, not on the roof man, put it in the food zone! Anyway, it's got to be tinned if it's going to survive ten years of fallout!

In terms of more serious television, who will ever forget *Edge Of Darkness*? First shown on the BBC in 1985, it followed the journey of a police inspector, Ronald Craven, trying to come to terms with his daughter's death. He ends up caught up in a conspiracy about environmental terrorism, plutonium, and the Knights of St John as a secret underground plant reprocesses waste from power plants into weapons-grade material.

Filmed largely in a disused Welsh mine, it was written by *Z Cars* man Troy Kennedy Martin, starred the late Bob Peck and included music by Eric Clapton. It was quickly repeated and his since taken on cult status, with tribute websites revealing marvellous trivia about it including the fact in the original ending, Craven becomes a tree. If ever there was a nuclear power equivalent to *Threads*, it was *Edge Of Darkness*.

Another drama written by Troy Kennedy Martin was *The Old Men At The Zoo*. This allegorical drama, based on a novel by Angus Wilson, focussed on the build up to a nuclear war as seen through the goings-on at a zoo. As soon as war is inevitable, the 'dangerous species' are destroyed. It culminates in a fascist government taking power and the rebellion movement adopting a stuffed Yeti as their leader. 'I must say, I think the Foreign Office has made a frightful mess of it this time,' observes a civil servant as the missiles reach England.

For a comprehensive, witty and clever overview of the influence of nuclear paranoia on early Cold War America, look no further than *The Atomic Café*. Correctly dubbed 'the blackest apocalyptic humour since *Dr Strangelove*' by the Washington Post, it was a triumphant collage of nuclear and Cold War paranoia from the 1950s. Composed mainly by clips from American government propaganda films, including Duck And Cover, it sends up the sort of misinformation that characterised discussion of nuclear war during this time.

When you think about nuclear war, you think about visualise mushroom clouds, babies being vaporised or ruined cities. You don't often think about the world of fashion but nuclear war has had more of an influence than you might think on the world of clothing and style. In 1946, French fashion designer Louis Reard was looking for a name for a new range of women's bathing clothes he had invented. Up until the mid-1940s, the smallest bathing suit for women was known as 'the atom'. So when Reard designed an even skimpier outfit, he had effectively smashed the atom. Just four days before the launch of his new outfit, the US Military conducted nuclear tests on the Bikini Atoll, a string of islands in the Pacific. Reard seized the moment and capitalized on the hype about the tests by naming his outfit the bikini.

But the most famous instance of nuclear fashion is the good old CND logo. One of the most widely recognized symbols in the world, it was designed in 1958 by Gerald Holtom. A graduate of the Royal College of Arts, he produced a few preliminary sketches of the logo and showed them to a few peace movement groups including the Direct Action Committee Against Nuclear War, a forerunner for CND.

Having got the nod for the logo, the first badges were produced by CND member Eric Austin who used white clay, with the symbol painted on in black. With symbolic flourish, the leaflets that were distributed along with this first run of badges explained that these pottery badges would be among the only human artefacts to survive a nuclear war.

But what did the symbol mean? Gerald Holtom it incorporated the semaphore letters for 'n' and 'd' – nuclear disarmament. He also says: 'I was in despair. Deep despair. I drew myself: the representative of an individual in despair, with hands palm outstretched outwards and downwards in the manner of Goya's peasant before the firing squad. I formalised the drawing into a line and put a circle round it.'

Of all instances of nuclear paranoia in popular culture, across music, television, literature and fashion, one surely stands out. A moment of epochal importance in the cultural history of nuclear paranoia, confirming how central this fear has become in our existence, our imagination. I write, of course, of *The Simpsons*.

Homer J Simpson, father of Bart, is the safety inspector at the Springfield Nuclear Power Plant. The donut-scoffing, beer-swilling bowler tosses pieces of nuclear waste out of his card window as he drives home at night from the plant, which is held together by pieces of chewing gum. He uses plutonium rods as paperweights and leaves key areas unmanned.

In 2001, the Nuclear Energy Institute was so concerned by the decline in nuclear power's popularity among the US public, it launched an advertisement campaign to help promote it. The same year, a New South Wales MP who was opposing the Australian government's plans to build a new nuclear reactor in the area said: 'It's just a crazy suggestion, I mean Mr Burns would love it,' referring to *The Simpsons* character.

Matt Groening, creator of *The Simpsons* who once worked in sewage treatment centre near a nuclear power station in Oregon, has handed the anti-nuclear power movement a huge gift in Homer J Simpson. Why bother telling people about the environmental impact and deaths that resulted from Chernobyl and Three Mile Island when the words Homer J Simpson say all you need to about the dangers of nuclear power.

8. Whoops, apocalypse!: Chernobyl, the millennium bug and a host of near-misses

When they went back to clean up afterwards, one of the first things they had to do was shoot the wildlife that remained. Everywhere they looked, they saw animals and birds either blind, dead or dying. Nikolai Goshchitsky was involved in the clean-up and remembers: 'They crawled, half alive, along the road, in terrible pain. Birds looked as if they had crawled out of water, unable to fly or walk. Cats with dirty fur, as if it had been burnt in places.'

In the early hours of Saturday, 26th April, 1986, an explosion blew the lid off the no. 4 reactor at the Chernobyl nuclear power plant in the Ukraine. Radioactive debris was thrown over a large area. The Soviet authorities failed to grasp the gravity of the situation initially. Two days later, a Swedish monitoring station detected abnormally high levels of radiation – only then did the Soviets even admit that an accident had occurred.

Too little, too late: volunteers who had been cleaning up the leaked radiation had done so without protective clothing - most were soon in hospital and many died. Some had radioactive vapour burnt into their lungs, many lay in agony as their internal organs began to disintegrate. Even in death, they suffered. Special concrete slabs were placed under their coffins, to stop their still radioactive bodies from infecting the soil.

Too little, too late: it was days before an evacuation was organised – but not before many had been exposed to a dose of radiation between 100 and 200 times more powerful than that from the Hiroshima bomb.

The radiation spread around the globe. Sweden, Poland, Germany and Austria were badly effected. Huge quantities of milk and vegetable produce had to be destroyed, (a setback that was preferable to what happened in Chernobyl itself, where meat workers at a local factory recall contaminated meat, including cattle whose internal organs were black and rotten, still being sold to the local population.) Rain brought down radioactive particles across Wales, Northern England and Scotland.

Officially, 41 people died as a result of the Chernobyl disaster, but scientists estimate the figure could have been higher if you included those troops taken to military hospitals, whose deaths were not disclosed. In June 1987, three of the Chernobyl power plant's staff were put on trial, found guilty violations of discipline and regulations causing human injury and other grevious consequences, and sentenced to ten year's in prison. The trial was held in Chernobyl, and there were pans of water at the court entrance in which visitors were meant to wash the soles of their shoes. All lawyers taking part in the trial were advised to shower twice a day.

Perhaps the single most depressing legacy of the disaster came in the shape of a boy, Igor, who was conceived two months after the accident. He was born with no right arms and tiny legs, just one symbol of the increase in genetic disorders among the local population, many of whom were abandoned into run-down orphanages. He now lives in Surrey, England with a foster family.

In the early hours of Wednesday 28th March, reactor 2 of the Three Mile Island nuclear plant in Pennsylvania, almost produced a catastrophe. A number of faults occurred in the reactor and as workers tried to rescue the situation, some hydrogen escaped into the building. Suddenly, the room started shaking and there was a loud bang as the hydrogen in the building exploded. Had the hydrogen bubble inside the reactor also exploded, the results would have been catastrophic.

The company that owned the plant, Metropolitan Edison, assured the public that everything was under control. Few believed them. High levels of radiation were recorded above the plant, local people drove out of the area. Pennsylvania State Governor Richard Thornburg recommended that pregnant women and school children living within an eight kilometre radius of the plant should leave the area.

Plans were put in place for an official evacuation of a thirty-two kilometre zone around the plant, which would have included 650,000 people including the residents of a local hospital and prison. Luckily, the crisis was under control before this had to happen.

In 1957, Britain had its own nuclear accident when a fire broke out at the Windscale plant in Cumbria (now renamed Sellafield). Initial attempts to control the fire were abject failures. Fans were switched on, but instead of calming the fire they made it worse. Carbon dioxide was pumped in to cool the fire, but this also failed. Engineers were faced with a dilemma. They could flood the effected area with water but there was a real risk this could lead to a huge nuclear explosion. They took the risk and it brought the fire under control.

No warning was given to local people as the fire had raged. It was claimed that any radiation was being carried out to sea by the wind but the wind changed direction, the result being that radioactive material rising out of the plant was carried over England, Ireland and other parts of Europe. It has been estimated that 95 people would die of cancer as a result of the fire but the official history of the disaster, published in 1987, has been criticised by some victims.

Jenny Uglow was a pupil at a local school at the time of the fire. She wrote a letter to *The Guardian* newspaper thirty years later. 'Our daily walk was along the cinder track towards the power station; and we all drank milk. On the night of the fire my father was fishing for sea-trout in the shadow of Windscale (he thought the men in the fields with torches were poachers!) A few years later my mother had severe thyroid problems and she was later operated on (successfully) for cancer. Next my father developed chronic, soon fatal kidney failure. We all know many, many people in the neighbourhood who have died young of cancer. Will this be part of the 'official history', or do we have to tell our own? It has proven extremely difficult for ordinary people to contact the researchers: to whom should we submit the evidence?'

If buckpassing, scapegoating and cover-ups are the order of the day for accidents involving nuclear power stations, one wonders just how much we don't know about accidents involving nuclear missiles. Before we turn to what we do know, are we agreed that when it comes to accidents involving nuclear weapons, our governments probably only allow us to hear the half of it?

On July 26th 1957, a US B-47 plane was practising a landing at an RAF base near Cambridge. The pilot lost control and the plane smashed into a storage building – a storage building that housed three nuclear bombs. The planes fuel threatened to ignite the TNT in the trigger mechanism of the bombs but fire-fighters were able to prevent disaster.

The following year, another US B-47 accidentally dropped a nuclear weapon into the garden of Walter Gregg, who lived in South Carolina. Luckily for everyone in the area, it was an unarmed nuclear missile. Unfortunately for Gregg, the conventional explosion it caused destroyed his house and injured six of his family. Six other buildings, including a church, were also damaged. He received $54,000 in compensation.

In on January 17th, 1966, a US B-52 bomber was flying 30,000 feet over the Mediterranean coast. It collided with a jet tanker, which had arrived to refuel it, and in the explosion that followed four hydrogen bombs fell from the B-52, heading straight for the Spanish village of Palomares.

Although safety devices prevented the bombs from completely exploding, two of them did rupture, spreading radioactive particles over hundreds of acres of the farmland of Palomares. A third landed intact, while the fourth landed in the sea and was later found after a huge, frantic search.

The US government immediately announced that there was: 'no danger to public health or safety as a result of this accident.' In fact, nearly 1,750 metric tons of radioactive soil had to be removed for burial at a US nuclear waste dump and several tons of tomato crops had to be destroyed.

On September 8th, 1977, a Soviet submarine accidentally jettisoned a nuclear warhead in the Pacific Ocean. On June 3rd 1980, a single computer chip failed in the NORAD detection operation. Consequently, a Soviet missile attack was mistakenly detected and 100 B-52 bombers were prepared for retaliation before the error was discovered.

The following year, a US submarine carrying 160 nuclear warheads collided with a Japanese freighter. In November 1981, a nuclear missile was being winched from a submarine onto a US ship. It was caught just before it hit the submarine. In the same month, a fully-armed Poseidon nuclear missile was accidentally dropped 17 feet from a crane in Scotland. Then on March 21st 1984, in the middle of the Reagan era, a US aircraft carrier armed with several dozen nuclear missiles collided with a Soviet attack submarine carrying nuclear armed torpedoes.

You would need a whole book to even begin to do justice to the amount of accidents involving nuclear weapons there have been since 1945. The above is only a selection, and even then only a selection of those the governments concerned have not managed to hush-up. It's a truly terrifying tale.

And a tale with its own language. The US military refer to any incident involving a nuclear weapon or warhead as a 'broken arrow', with the weapon or warhead concerned referred to as a 'bent spear'. If the incident involves the seizure, theft or loss of a nuclear missile, the incident is referred as an 'empty quiver'. Meanwhile, an incident involving a nuclear power station is referred to as a 'faded giant'.

So typical are these terms of the wonderfully understated world of nuclear lingo. As we've seen, the world's first atomic bomb, which Oppenheimer's team tested in New Mexico, was called 'the gadget'. The first atomic bomb used in anger, when it was dropped on Hiroshima, was called 'Little Boy'. Now, we have nuclear accidents called broken arrows and bent spears. The men behind the nuclear dictionary have a great sense of humour.

Although, at the time of writing, none of these accidents have caused an all-out nuclear explosion, some have come agonisingly close. On 24th January, 1961, two 25-megaton nuclear missiles were released after a B-52 bomber broke apart in mid-air over North Carolina. One bomb parachuted to safety but the other landed in a waterlogged area of farmland. When it was found, it was discovered that five of the six safety devices built into it had failed – and we'd come within a whisker of a bomb one thousand times more powerful than the Hiroshima bomb, exploding.

Even these near-misses have serious environmental consequences. On 22nd January, 1968, a US B-52 crashed into ice seven miles south of Thule Air Force Base in Greenland and exploded. The four hydrogen bombs on board scattered radioactive debris over the area. The people and government of Denmark were outraged, as Greenland was a province of theirs at the time and Denmark prided itself on being a nuclear-free zone. After this incident, the US government decided to end these flights.

One of the warheads involved in this accident was reportedly recovered from the sea in 1979, but a report published in August 2000 suggests it may still be lying in the ocean. If so, it would be one of over 50 nuclear warheads which environmentalists claim lie scattered along the bottom of the world's oceans.

The turning of the millennium has always been associated with a sense of foreboding. Before the arrival of the year 1000, many predicted the end of the world and similar prophecies were widely made about the arrival of the year 2000 – only this time there was a technological background to the paranoia.

The millennium bug dates back to the 1960s when computer programmers began designating the year by using two digits rather than four, to conserve memory. As the new millennium approached, fears grew that widespread chaos could ensue when the world's computers failed to recognise the year 2000.

But chaos was the least of our worries when it came to the planet's nuclear arsenal, with the radars, satellites and triggering devices all theoretically at risk from the millennium bug. Could the new millennium be ushered in with a huge nuclear firework display wiping out the planet?

The Ministry of Defence certainly thought this a possibility and spent an estimated £200 million in addressing the problem, while the US Department of Defence splashed a cool $3,700 million on it. Even with such massive expenditure, there was reason for concern. US Deputy Secretary of Defence John Hamre admitted: 'Probably one out of five days I wake up in a cold sweat thinking Y2K is much bigger than we think, and then the other four days I think maybe we really are on top of it. Everything is so inter-connected, it's hard to know with any precision whether we have got it fixed.'

The picture in the former Soviet Union was even less reassuring. Until February 1999, Russia's military leaders flatly denied that their nuclear forces could possibly face problems from the millennium bug. Most worrying was Russia's nuclear control system, called 'Perimeter' which ensured that if Moscow looked like it was under attack, or even if command links to key Russian leaders were interrupted, Perimeter would automatically launch thousands of nuclear weapons.

President Bill Clinton and Boris Yeltsin planned a joint US/Russian early warning centre, to help avoid catastrophic misunderstanding. This was re-assuring but then a US Defence Department worker was asked when the centre would be open. He said: 'We're hoping to have it done by late '99. It could be early 2000. It's a complex process, obviously.'

India, Pakistan, France, Israel and China revealed little about their own preparations but that which was known, suggested they were lagging far behind the superpowers. In China, for instance, it is estimated that over 90 per cent of the nation's software is pirated, which made it virtually impossible to acquire technical advice as to how to address the problem there.

In the end, it was widely argued that the only way to avoid catastrophe was for all nations to agree to de-arm their nuclear weapons during the danger period. None of the world's nuclear powers were willing to do this, so as we went into the millennium celebrations, all we could do was pray.

As it turned out, it was a happy new year rather than nuclear year and the only explosions witnessed were the firework displays which took place at the stroke of midnight. Yet again, our fears about a nuclear war scenario had proved misguided. Perhaps, we thought, nuclear paranoia really was just that: a paranoia. As we entered the new millennium we could put not just the millennium bug but the Cold War behind us. Nuclear war seemed a less likely prospect than ever. Maybe we could all stop worrying…

9. Just when you thought it was safe: 21st Century paranoia; nuclear terrorism; India and Pakistan

And then they flew those planes into the World Trade Centre and everything changed. No sooner had the twin towers collapsed and crashed to the ground than a new wave of nuclear paranoia gripped the planet. Did the terrorists responsible have access to weapons of mass destruction, including nuclear arms? Would George W Bush consider using nuclear arms if future acts of mass terrorism were committed against the US?

Meanwhile, what were previously distant, nagging nuclear head-aches became full-on migraines. Fears about the conflict between India and Pakistan and the continued menace of Saddam Hussein in Iraq took on a whole new urgency in the context of a war against terrorism.

Perhaps the most nagging nightmare was and is, the prospect of a gang of ruthless terrorists getting their hands on nuclear material. At the top of this list of fear, is Osama Bin Laden. The Saudi millionaire, head of Al Qaeda movement and sponsor of international terrorism including the September 11th attacks on New York and Washington, is thought to have been trying to obtain nuclear weapons since the early 1990s.

In 1993, Bin Laden sent a senior Al Qaeda lieutenant to a number of Central Asian states to meet potential sellers of nuclear material. The trips were a spectacular failure and a number of contacts seemed more interested in ripping off the Al Qaeda man. Later, Israeli intelligence learned of a potential deal being struck in Kazakhstan and immediately intervened to stop the deal going through.

Under Taliban rule, there was a black market in Afghanistan that was awash with uranium and other nuclear material, much of it stolen from the former Soviet Union. There are still reports of thefts and attempted thefts at former Soviet nuclear sites to this day. Such materials could be used to construct a 'dirty bomb' – a conventional explosive packed with radioactive waste. When exploded, such a device would spread radiation over a large area.

Later in the 1990s, Bin Laden was rumoured to have given Chechen mafia agents several million pounds in cash together with £300 million in heroin to obtain nuclear suitcase bombs for Al Qaeda. According to senior US intelligence sources, these weapons were handed to Bin Laden in autumn 1998, whereupon he stashed them in Taliban complex near Kandahar in Afghanistan.

The whereabouts of them since the September 11 US bombing of Afghanistan is unknown. However, during the campaign at least one piece of evidence was uncovered. When Allied forces entered an abandoned Al Qaeda camp in Afghanistan they discovered a mass of literature, including a guide to how to build a crude nuclear weapon. While this sent a wave of panic through the Western world, some believed it a little too convenient that Al Qaeda happened to leave such a document lying around where they knew Allied forces would search. Was this evidence of a nuclear plot or merely an act of propaganda?

Weeks on from that discovery, reports surfaced of an Al Qaeda man waving a canister of nuclear material in the air at a meeting in Afghanistan. It has also emerged that in the months leading up to the September 11th attacks, Bin Laden held a meeting with two retired Pakistani nuclear scientists about the building of nuclear weapons and also met with a Bulgarian businessman to offer him a role in a plan to send nuclear waste to Afghanistan.

Bin Laden has publicly stated his desire to obtain nuclear arms. 'We don't consider it a crime if we tried to have nuclear, chemical and biological weapons,' he says. 'Our holy land is occupied by Israeli and American forces. We have the right to defend ourselves and to liberate our holy land. Acquiring weapons for the defence of Muslims is a religious duty.'

On whether his atomic forays have been successful, the Saudi is teasingly coy. 'If I have indeed acquired these weapons, then I thank God for enabling me to do so. And if I seek to acquire these weapons, then I am carrying out a duty. It would be a sin for Muslims not to try to possess the weapons that would prevent infidels from inflicting harm on Muslims.'

For a few horrible minutes in 2002, a group of English school children fully believed that not only did Bin Laden possess nuclear arms but that he had just detonated one over the UK. Teachers at the Bushfield Community College in Peterborough told a drama class full of 15 and 16 year old pupils that Bin Laden had escaped from Afghanistan and launched a nuclear attack on Britain. The pupils were even encouraged to phone their parents and say their farewells.

Peterborough local education authority later apologised for the 'extremely unfortunate' misunderstanding which left many of the pupils in tears. At the beginning of the drama class, the pupils had been warned that, as was normal in this class, anything that happened would be fictitious and aimed to evoke emotional responses from the pupils.

But Bin Laden and company are not the only terrorists interested in going nuclear. The Russian government alone lists over 200 terrorist organisations it believes may be trying to buy nuclear material. Between 1998 and 2001, the Russian security services have intervened in over 600 attempted deals between terrorists and rogue agents selling nuclear material.

In Japan, the apocalyptic Aum Shinrikyo cult, responsible for the 1995 sarin attack on five Tokyo subway trains, has been on the nuclear trail since the early 1990s. The group has actively attempted to recruit unemployed Russian nuclear experts, as well as students from the Moscow State University. It has also purchased land in Australia, on which it planned to mine natural uranium. In 1993, it even audaciously attempted to set up a meeting with the then Russian Energy Minister, Viktor Mikhailov, to discuss the possibility of purchasing a nuclear bomb. Mikhailov refused to meet them.

But since September 11th, it has become clear that terrorists could mount a nuclear attack using nothing more advanced than a hijacked airliner. There are fears that the Al Qaeda could fly a plane into a nuclear power station. Some intelligence experts in the US believe that the intended destination for the fourth hijacked September 11th plane, which crashed in Pensylvania, was not the White House but a nuclear power reactor, such as Three Mile Island. Security experts have had to admit that England and America's nuclear power stations were not built to withstand the impact of a fully loaded jumbo jet.

This bombshell can be added to a crime-sheet of other disturbing facts about nuclear power station security. The US Nuclear Regulatory Commission (NRC) does not require operators of power stations to be prepared for more than three intruders, more than one team of attackers using co-ordinated tactics or any intruder using a weapon larger than hand-held automatic weapons.

During the 1990s, the NRC staged a counter-terrorist training programme for its members. Mock attacks would be staged to evaluate how nuclear power stations would cope in the event of a real terrorist act. Under the programme, the power stations would be given six month's warning of the exact date of the mock attack and were able to step up security accordingly. Even so, nearly half of the power stations failed the tests with the mock terrorists comfortably penetrating security.

In Britain in October 2001, amid growing fears of security at nuclear power stations, two Tornado fighter jets were reported to have been scrambled to patrol the sky over the Sellafield plant for several hours following a telephone threat. The disturbing vulnerability of nuclear power stations remains a worryingly unsolved security problem.

The following year, amid recriminations aimed at the FBI and CIA for their failure to foresee the September 11th attacks, the US authorities arrested a man they believed was plotting to detonate a nuclear 'dirty bomb' in Washington. Abdullah al-Mujahir, a US citizen who had recently converted to Islam, was described as an operative for Al Qaeda, and his arrest heightened fears about a possible terrorist attack using radioactive materials.

'Dirty bombs' are conventional bombs, packed with radioactive isotopes, which when exploded spread radioactive material over a wide area. A contaminated region could end up uninhabitable for years and the panic that such an attack would generate isn't hard to imagine.

We don't need to imagine the panic that al-Mujahir's arrest sparked because it was played out across the media. Once again, newspapers and magazines carried apocalyptic headlines. Experts queued up to offer ever more fearsome estimations of the death toll that a dirty bomb could inflict. Others speculated about the ease with which Al Qaeda could obtain radioactive material.

However, very quickly the threat was put in perspective. Paol Wolfowitz, US deputy defence secretary, was forced to admit that al-Mujahir's conspiracy had not as yet entailed 'an actual plan'. Other intelligence sources admitted that he'd done nothing more than surf a few websites dealing with explosives and discussed attacking a petrol station or hotel. And let's remember that despite month after month of searching through Al Qaeda safe-houses and mountain hideouts in Afghanistan, no actual radioactive material was ever found.

Amid all this rising panic, a strong, clear head was urgently needed. Enter, stage far-right, George W Bush, the man who spent part of the afternoon of September 11 in a nuclear bunker. In March 2002, a Pentagon report on the United States' nuclear plans was leaked to the media. Entitled the 'nuclear posture review', the document listed seven countries that the US now considers contenders for a nuclear assault. The unlucky seven were Russia, China, Iran, Iraq, Libya, North Korea and Syria.

Greeted with widespread horror, the report advocated first-use of nuclear weapons in a number of scenarios. These included an Iraqi attack on Israel or Kuwait, a North Korean invasion of South Korea, or a military assault on Taiwan by China. Immediately, China expressed its shock and, along with Russia, demanded an explanation from Washington. The Iranian government, meanwhile, made clear its disgust by accusing the US government of being no better than terrorists.

Although it was only natural for these governments to feel alarm, the news that Bush was thinking of nuking them must have really ruined their day, the report only really removed a little ambiguity from the United States' nuclear policy. Ever since the Gulf War of 1991, when the United States and Britain issued thinly-veiled threats that if Saddam Hussein used chemical weapons on Allied troops that he would face the force of their nuclear fury, United States policy has been moving in this direction. All that had really changed was that the US didn't previously make a habit of naming specific countries as nuclear targets, or at least not publicly.

Perhaps the background to this new policy was a belief that just as nuclear weapons helped deter World War Three during the Cold War era, there was no surer way of deterring the likes of Iraq, North Korea or terrorists like Al Qaeda, than threatening to blow them apart with a few nuclear bombs. Quite how this policy was meant to discourage bitter enemies of the United States from acquiring or even using nuclear arms themselves is something that George W Bush has yet to outline.

Another troubling aspect of this new posture was Bush's plans to construct smaller nuclear weapons that could burrow underground and destroy bunkers, hidden facilities of buried chemical weapon stores. Meanwhile, in England, similar moves were afoot. It was revealed that a new bomb-making factory was being planned in Aldermaston. The plant was designed to build a new generation of nuclear arms. These would be smaller atomic warheads for use against terrorist groups and rogue states. These plans were revealed hot on the heels of British Defence Secretary Geoff Hoon's insistence that Britain has a right to use nuclear arms pre-emptively against states that are not themselves nuclear powers.

The most disturbing element of these developments on both sides of the Atlantic was that it seemed the public were being slowly brought round to the idea that the use of nuclear weapons was no longer an unimaginable or, necessarily, catastrophic scenario. The very fact that Bush and Blair were planning to build smaller nuclear weapons suggested an increase in the nuclear threat. What better way to usher in a new era where nuclear attack is deemed acceptable than to introduce smaller nuclear arms and claim that they're nothing to be scared of?

Not that Bush considers himself at all short of justification since September 11th. The attacks on the World Trade Centre terrified America and made the public feel more vulnerable than ever – the perfect pretext for Bush to go after whoever he wanted. The threat of the Soviet Union during the Cold war had never been as visible somehow. How could we visualise this threat? No such problems with the new threats to Western security, the threat of Al Qaeda is as easy to picture as possible, given news broadcasters' love affair with those images of airliners crashing into the Twin Towers, of people jumping out of windows, of the buildings collapsing.

In such an atmosphere, who was to hold Bush back as he attempted to settle scores? And on both a political and personal level, Saddam Hussein must constitute one of Bush's biggest scores to settle. The Iraqi leader also remains at the epicentre of the new wave of nuclear paranoia. Saddam has been trying to build a nuclear arsenal for Iraq since the 1970s, when he first hired a team of scientists and ordered them to construct a device equivalent to the bomb dropped on Hiroshima. He set them a production target of six bombs a year and at times employed up to 12,000 people on the project.

Given that revenge against the United States must figure pretty highly on Saddam's 'to-do' list, there is a certain irony in the first breakthrough the project enjoyed. The scientists' first lesson on uranium enrichment were garnered from the Manhattan Project's reports, which were given as a gift to Iraq in the 1950s, complete with the greeting: 'This is a gift from the US Atomic Energy Commission.'

To the best of our knowledge, the project has never come to atomic fruition. But it has come perilously close. In 1975, one of its leading lights arranged a meeting with the authorities at Atomic Energy of Canada Limited. He was seeking, on Saddam's orders, to buy a nuclear reactor for Iraq. His order was rejected not on moral or safety grounds, rather that the Canadians had too heavy a backlog of orders to take on any new ones. Phew.

Later, just prior to his 1990 invasion of Kuwait, Saddam became especially anxious to see the construction of at least one nuclear device completed. He ordered a crash programme to produce a war-head that he could mount on a conventional missile and fire at Israel if the Allied troops came directly after him. He was quite clear that if he was going down, everyone in the region was going down with him.

To say George W Bush, son of Saddam's 1991 Gulf War adversary George Bush, is keen to see the dictator off is something of an understatement. He spent much of 2002 talking up the possibility that Iraq is at least very close to having nuclear arms, together with chemical bombs and other weapons of mass destruction.

The possibility of a United States v Iraq dust-up ending in at least one of the sides using nuclear arms was a real possibility in 2002. But there was a far bigger nuclear nightmare troubling the planet that year. Although it never rivalled the Cuban Missile Crisis for white-knuckle tension, the stand-off between India and Pakistan kept us pretty close to the edges of our seats throughout the year. Plenty of commentators had long been expressing grave concern about the arms race on the Indian sub-continent, but it was only in the wake of the September 11th attacks that the wider world sat up and took the matter seriously.

India and Pakistan have been squabbling over control of Kashmir since they became independent in 1947. More recently, since 1989, Indian forces in Indian-held Kashmir have faced a violent uprising. Then, in the wake of September 11, the conflict took on a whole new urgency as India demanded that Pakistan join the 'war on terror' spirit by seriously cracking down on Pakistan-based Islamic militants.

There followed a series of battles across the frontline of the conflict, with both sides regularly shelling one another. After the Indian parliament building was attacked in December 2001, both sides talk became increasingly and worryingly aggressive. Then, as if the population didn't have enough to trouble them, Tony Blair flew in at the start of January 2002, to express his wish that peace would prevail between the two countries. (A month later, the British government tried to sell arms to India which rather undermined the sincerity of Blair's peace mission but that's another book.)

Far from listening to Blair's pleas for peace, the tension in the area steadily mounted. By May 2002, up to a million troops were gathered around the border, replacing thousands of civilians who had fled the area. Among this number were many Briton, who left on the advice of Foreign Secretary Jack Straw MP who told them to leave for their own safety. This advice followed similar words from the United States government, who also pulled all non-essential diplomats from the region and advised all Americans living in the area to get the hell out.

India always insisted it would not use nuclear weapons first but Pakistan was quite clear that it would. However, Western diplomats in the region felt India could quite easily push the button first. After so much sabre-rattling by the Indian government, it was feared that they might fire first merely not to appear to be all-talk.

There was also grave concern that the fear of losing their nuclear arsenal during a conventional war, if their opponents bombed their nuclear bases, gave rise to concern that either side might drop their nuclear bombs on the other merely to avoid losing them. It was estimated that India had up to 150 nuclear warheads and Pakistan anywhere between 10 and 100.

Around the world, the media adored the crisis. Kashmir was dubbed 'the new Cuba' as the tension mounted. Newspapers, magazines and television shows around the world predicted the worst. *India Today*, a weekly magazine, predicted that New Delhi would become a mammoth graveyard if hit by a nuclear strike from Pakistan. Meanwhile, it said, any Indian retaliation would wipe out Islamabad and other Pakistani population centres. The feature was illustrated with gratuitous images of the devastation inflicted on Hiroshima and Nagasaki. It concluded with the prediction that Pakistan itself would ultimately disappear and over 12 million people would perish if nuclear war broke out.

Closer to home, *The Daily Mail* published a full page feature entitled: 'So what would happen if they pushed the button?' Illustrated with a huge photograph of a mushroom cloud, it predicted: 'The centre of New Delhi is reduced to a swirl of atoms, and maybe a million people are dead…The President, Prime Minister and Cabinet are vaporised. Nevertheless, out in the deserts of the north west, the military men have their orders and an hour later, India takes its revenge.

'Three Agni Mk2 missiles…will head towards Islamabad, Lahore and Karachi. As a result of this apocalyptic tit-for-tat, 12 million people will be dead, seven million more gravely injured and tens of millions made homeless.'

The further into the feature you read, the more you had to remind yourself that this was *The Daily Mail* you were reading and not a scaremongering CND recruitment leaflet. The feature also predicted a huge humanitarian crisis and warned that radioactive fallout from the region could reach as far as Britain.

Even the BBC couldn't resist a little dark speculation. 'World War Three could be just around the corner,' its website wrote. 'With China siding with Pakistan and the United States with India.'

Elsewhere in cyberspace, some had a more light-hearted take on the crisis. 'The Indo-Pakistani Deadpool' website boasted that it was 'Exploiting the coming nuclear holocaust for fun and profit!' It was essentially offering visitors the chance to place a spread-bet on when the first nuclear bomb would be used in the region. As a tie-breaker, in the event that two punters chose the same correct date, contestants were also asked to predict the number of people that would die in the war.

The contest rules pointed out that if the winning contestant was actually killed in the nuclear war, his or her family would not be able to claim the prize on their behalf. It also ruled that members of the Indian and Pakistani governments would not be allowed to enter. 'Too easy to cheat,' it explained. Quite.

While some visitors complained bitterly that the site marked a new low in lack of Internet taste, it could equally be argued that the mainstream media were no less exploitative of the crisis with their 'panic stations' stories. There was a deep irony in the fact that the very same media which had previously sneered at the anti-nuclear movement for predicting a nuclear war and speculating about the likely effects of one, now indulged in exactly the same orgy of mushroom cloud imagery, death estimates and fallout figures.

How must veteran anti-nuclear campaigner Michael Foot, who published a superb book: *Dr Strangelove, I Presume*, warning of the dangers of the India/Pakistan arms race in 1999 to widespread snorts of derision have felt as he saw mainstream, right-wing newspapers fall over themselves to warn their readers of the danger?

So how to sum up this new era of nuclear paranoia and place it in the context of past panics? In many ways, nuclear war seems more obtainable than it ever has. Even as we worried that Reagan and Thatcher would start a nuclear war, or while the world sat on the edge of their seats during the thirteen days of the Cuban missile crisis, there remained at least the sense that these leaders had a lot to lose were they to press the button.

It's not quite as easy to believe that terrorists, with their death wishes and furiously raging sense of injustice, feel they have much to lose. Where is the sense that Bin Laden and his disciples have any sense of restraint? And will the US, led by George W Bush, accept many further provocations along the lines of September 11, before it truly lashes out with the big one?

The world sure feels a lot less safe right now. Perhaps, though, September 11 did in one sense make nuclear war less likely. All these years, we've waited for the big disaster and act of war to happen and when it did, it was delivered not through a nuclear bomb but with nothing more powerful than a few cardboard cutting knives on some US passenger planes.

Just how does one measure the nuclear threat? What is the barometer of the bomb? Perhaps the Doomsday Clock, maintained by the Bulletin of Atomic Scientists, is perhaps the best primer of the current state of play in terms of the nuclear threat. Since 1947, it has been the most potent symbol of nuclear danger as the minute hand moved closer to midnight, or doomsday, when the threat has increased and then been moved back again during happier times.

For instance, in 1953, it stood at just two minutes to midnight as the United States and Russia tested nuclear bombs within months of each other and the nuclear arms race gathered a sinister pace. After moving out as far as twelve minutes to midnight, it ominously zoomed back in to three minutes to in 1984, as Reagan and company pressed the arms race accelerator right down.

By 1991, we could all breathe more easily as arms cut treaties between the United States and Russia saw the minute hand move out to seventeen minutes, the furthest from midnight it had ever been.

In mid-2002, the clock stood at seven minutes to midnight. So, while the nuclear threat has markedly increased over the past decade, we're not yet back to darkest days of the Cold War arms race.

But that clock is always ticking…

Bibliography

Einstein's Monsters, Martin Amis, 1987, Vintage. ISBN 0 09 976891 7

London After The Bomb, Owen Greene et al, 1982. ISBN 0 19 285123 3

Brother In The Land, Robert Swindells, Puffin, 1984. ISBN 0 14 037300 4

With Enough Shovels: Reagan, Bush & Nuclear War, Robert Scheer, Secker & Warburg, 1982. ISBN 0 436 44355 4

The Nuclear Age – From Hiroshima to Star Wars, John Newhouse, Michael Joseph, 1989. ISBN 07181 32637

Chernobyl And Other Nuclear Accidents, Judith Condon, Hodder Wayland, 1998, ISBN 0750221704.

The New Jackals: Osama Bin Laden And The Future Of Terrorism, Simon Reeve, Carlton Books, 2001. ISBN 0233050485.

Dr Strangelove I Presume, Michael Foot, Orion, July 2002. ISBN 0753809249.

Millennium Movies, Kim Newman, Titan Books, 1999. ISBN 1 84023 060 6

Cold War, Jeremy Isaacs and Taylor Downing, Bantam Press, 1998. ISBN 059304309X

Hiroshima, John Hersey, Penguin, 1985. ISBN 0 14 01 8291 8

Nuclear War Films, Jack G Shaheen (ED), Southern Illinois University Press, 1978. ISBN 0 8093 0879 7

Oppenheimer And The Bomb, Paul Strathern, Arrow, 1998. ISNB 0 09923792X

The Cuban Missile Crisis, Peter Chrisp, Hodder Wayland, 2001. ISBN 0750233893.

The Secret State, The Penguin Press, Peter Hennessy, 2002. ISBN 0713996269

Saddam's Bombmaker, Khidhir Hamza, Simon & Schuster, 2002. ISBN 0743211359

Your Face Here, Ali Catterall and Simon Wells, Fourth Estate, 2001. ISBN 184115203X.

The Essential Library: History Best-Sellers

Build up your library with new titles published every month

Conspiracy Theories by Robin Ramsay, £3.99

Do you think *The X-Files* is fiction? That Elvis is dead? That the US actually went to the moon? And don't know that the ruling elite did a deal with the extra-terrestrials after the Roswell crash in 1947... At one time, you could blame the world's troubles on the Masons or the Illuminati, or the Jews, or One Worlders, or the Great Communist Conspiracy. Now we also have the alien-US elite conspiracy, or the alien shape-shifting reptile conspiracy to worry about - and there are books to prove it as well! This book tries to sort out the handful of wheat from the choking clouds of intellectual chaff. For among the nonsensical Conspiracy Theory rubbish currently proliferating on the Internet, there are important nuggets of real research about real conspiracies waiting to be mined.

The Rise Of New Labour by Robin Ramsay, £3.99

The rise of New Labour? How did that happen? As everybody knows, Labour messed up the economy in the 1970s, went too far to the left, became 'unelectable' and let Mrs Thatcher in. After three General Election defeats Labour modernised, abandoned the left and had successive landslide victories in 1997 and 2001.

That's the story they print in newspapers. The only problem is...the real story of the rise of New Labour is more complex, and it involves the British and American intelligence services, the Israelis and elite management groups like the Bilderbergers.

Robin Ramsay untangles the myths and shows how it really happened that Gordon Brown sank gratefully into the arms of the bankers, Labour took on board the agenda of the City of London, and that nice Mr Blair embraced his role as the last dribble of Thatcherism down the leg of British politics.

UFOs by Neil Nixon, £3.99

UFOs and Aliens have been reported throughout recorded time. Reports of UFO incidents vary from lights in the sky to abductions. The details are frequently terrifying, always baffling and occasionally hilarious. This book includes the best known cases, the most incredible stories and the answers that explain them. There are astounding and cautionary tales which suggest that the answers we seek may be found in the least likely places.

The Essential Library: Film Best-Sellers

Build up your library with new titles every month

Stanley Kubrick by Paul Duncan

Kubrick's work, like all masterpieces, has a timeless quality. His vision is so complete, the detail so meticulous, that you believe you are in a three-dimensional space displayed on a two-dimensional screen. He was commercially successful because he embraced traditional genres like War (*Paths Of Glory*, *Full Metal Jacket*), Crime (*The Killing*), Science Fiction (*2001*), Horror (*The Shining*) and Love (*Barry Lyndon*). At the same time, he stretched the boundaries of film with controversial themes: underage sex (*Lolita*); ultra violence (*A Clockwork Orange*); and erotica (*Eyes Wide Shut*).

Film Noir by Paul Duncan

The laconic private eye, the corrupt cop, the heist that goes wrong, the femme fatale with the rich husband and the dim lover - these are the trademark characters of Film Noir. This book charts the progression of the Noir style as a vehicle for film-makers who wanted to record the darkness at the heart of American society as it emerged from World War to the Cold War. As well as an introduction explaining the origins of Film Noir, seven films are examined in detail and an exhaustive list of over 500 Films Noirs are listed.

Alfred Hitchcock by Paul Duncan

More than 20 years after his death, Alfred Hitchcock is still a household name, most people in the Western world have seen at least one of his films, and he popularised the action movie format we see every week on the cinema screen. He was both a great artist and dynamite at the box office. This book examines the genius and enduring popularity of one of the most influential figures in the history of the cinema!

Orson Welles by Martin Fitzgerald

The popular myth is that after the artistic success of *Citizen Kane* it all went downhill for Orson Welles, that he was some kind of fallen genius. Yet, despite overwhelming odds, he went on to make great Films Noirs like *The Lady From Shanghai* and *Touch Of Evil*. He translated Shakespeare's work into films with heart and soul (*Othello*, *Chimes At Midnight*, *Macbeth*), and he gave voice to bitterness, regret and desperation in *The Magnificent Ambersons* and *The Trial*. Far from being down and out, Welles became one of the first cutting-edge independent film-makers.

The Essential Library: Currently Available

Film Directors:

Woody Allen (2nd)	Tim Burton	Ang Lee
Jane Campion*	John Carpenter	Joel & Ethan Coen (2nd)
Jackie Chan	Steven Soderbergh	Clint Eastwood
David Cronenberg	Terry Gilliam*	Michael Mann
Alfred Hitchcock (2nd)	Krzysztof Kieslowski*	Roman Polanski
Stanley Kubrick (2nd)	Sergio Leone	Oliver Stone
David Lynch (2nd)	Brian De Palma*	George Lucas
Sam Peckinpah*	Ridley Scott (2nd)	James Cameron
Orson Welles (2nd)	Billy Wilder	Roger Corman
Steven Spielberg	Mike Hodges	Spike Lee
Hal Hartley		

Film Genres:

Blaxploitation Films	Bollywood	French New Wave
Horror Films	Spaghetti Westerns	Vietnam War Movies
Slasher Movies	Film Noir	Hammer Films
Vampire Films*	Heroic Bloodshed*	Carry On Films
German Expressionist Films		

Film Subjects:

Laurel & Hardy	Marx Brothers	Film Music
Steve McQueen*	Marilyn Monroe	The Oscars® (2nd)
Filming On A Microbudget	Bruce Lee	Writing A Screenplay
Film Studies		

Music:

The Madchester Scene	Beastie Boys	Jethro Tull
How To Succeed In The Music Business		The Beatles

Literature:

Cyberpunk	Philip K Dick	The Beat Generation
Agatha Christie	Sherlock Holmes	Noir Fiction
Terry Pratchett	Hitchhiker's Guide (2nd)	Alan Moore
William Shakespeare	Creative Writing	Tintin
Georges Simenon		

Ideas:

Conspiracy Theories	Nietzsche	UFOs
Feminism	Freud & Psychoanalysis	Bisexuality

History:

Alchemy & Alchemists	The Crusades	The Black Death
Jack The Ripper	The Rise Of New Labour	Ancient Greece
American Civil War	American Indian Wars	Witchcraft
Globalisation	Who Shot JFK?	

Miscellaneous:

Stock Market Essentials	How To Succeed As A Sports Agent	Doctor Who
Classic Radio Comedy		

Available at bookstores or send a cheque (payable to 'Oldcastle Books') to: **Pocket Essentials (Dept NP), P O Box 394, Harpenden, Herts, AL5 1XJ, UK.** £3.99 each (£2.99 if marked with an *). For each book add 50p(UK)/£1 (elsewhere) postage & packing